YOUR FAITH IS YOUR FORTUNE

AND

THE CREATIVE USE OF IMAGINATION

Neville Goddard

C L A S S Y
PUBLISHING

YOUR FAITH IS YOUR FORTUNE AND THE CREATIVE USE OF IMAGINATION
by Neville Goddard

Published by Classy Publishing, 2023

www.classypublishing.com
info@classypublishing.com

ISBN: 978-93-5522-643-3

No part of this publication may be reproduced, stored in a retrieval system, or transmitted, in any form or by any means, electronic, mechanical, photocopying, recording or otherwise, without the prior permission of the publisher.

Cover Design by Classy Publishing

Man's faith in God is measured by his confidence in himself.
—Neville Goddard

CONTENTS

YOUR FAITH IS YOUR FORTUNE

1.	Before Abraham Was	3
2.	You Shall Decree	5
3.	The Principle of Truth	9
4.	Whom Seek Ye?	16
5.	Who Am I?	24
6.	I Am He	33
7.	Thy Will Be Done	41
8.	No Other God	46
9.	The Foundation Stone	50
10.	To Him That Hath	53
11.	Christmas	56
12.	Crucifixion & Resurrection	60
13.	The I'm-Pressions	65
14.	Circumcision	69
15.	Interval of Time	72
16.	The Triune God	76
17.	Prayer	79
18.	The Twelve Disciples	82
19.	Liquid Light	91
20.	The Breath of Life	93
21.	Daniel in the Lions' Den	96
22.	Fishing	99
23.	Be Ears That Hear	102
24.	Clairvoyance	106
25.	Twenty Third Psalm	111
26.	Gethsemane	114
27.	A Formula for Victory	119

THE CREATIVE USE OF IMAGINATION

1. Your Infinite Worth — 129
2. Take Not the Name in Vain — 133
3. Desire — 137
4. Are You Making Wine? — 141
5. Seeing God — 143
6. All Is Consciousness — 147
7. Righteousness — 152
8. The Perfect Will of God — 156
9. Be Ye Doers of the Word — 160
10. The Pearl of Great Price — 164
11. Self-Remembering — 167
12. Your Destiny — 171
13. Your Personal Autobiography — 175
14. The Human Spirit — 181
15. The Feeling of "I" — 187
16. The Wine of Eternity — 191
17. Awake, O Sleeper — 196

YOUR FAITH IS YOUR FORTUNE

CHAPTER 1

Before Abraham Was

Verily, verily, I say unto you, before Abraham was, I AM.
—John 8:58

In the beginning was the Word, and the Word was with God, and the Word was God.
—John 1:1

In the beginning was the unconditioned awareness of being, and the unconditioned awareness of being became conditioned by imagining itself to be something, and the unconditioned awareness of being became that which it had imagined itself to be; so did creation begin.

By this law – first conceiving, then becoming that conceived – all things evolve out of No-thing; and without this sequence there is not anything made that is made.

Before Abraham or the world was – I AM. When all of time shall cease to be – I AM. I AM the formless awareness of being conceiving myself to be man. By my everlasting law of being I am compelled to be and to express all that I believe myself to be.

I AM the eternal No-thing-ness containing within my formless self the capacity to be all things.

I AM that in which all my conceptions of myself live and move and have their being, and apart from which they are not.

I dwell within every conception of myself; from this within-ness, I ever seek to transcend all conceptions of myself. By the very law of my being, I transcend my conceptions of myself, only as I believe myself to be that which does transcend.

I AM the law of being and beside ME there is no law. I AM that I AM.

CHAPTER 2

You Shall Decree

Thou shalt also decree a thing and it shall be established unto thee and the light shall shine upon thy ways.

You will also decree a thing, and it will be established for you; And light will shine on your ways. Thou shalt decree a thing, and it I shall come to thee, and light shall shine in thy ways.
—Job 22:28

So shall My word be that goeth forth out of My mouth; it shall not return unto Me void, but it shall accomplish that which I please, and it shall prosper in the thing whereto I sent it.
—Isaiah 55:11

Man can decree a thing and it will come to pass.

Man has always decreed that which has appeared in his world. He is today decreeing that which is appearing in his world and he shall continue to do so as long as man is conscious of being man.

Nothing has ever appeared in man's world, but what man decreed that it should. This you may deny; but try as you will, you cannot disprove it for this decreeing is based upon a changeless principle.

Man does not command things to appear by his words, which are, more often than not, a confession of his doubts and fears.

Decreeing is ever done in consciousness.

Every man automatically expresses that which he is conscious of being. Without effort or the use of words, at every moment of time, man is commanding himself to be and to possess that which he is conscious of being and possessing.

This changeless principle of expression is dramatized in all the Bibles of the world. The writers of our sacred books were illumined mystics, past masters in the art of psychology. In telling the story of the soul, they personified this impersonal principle in the form of a historical document both to preserve it and to hide it from the eyes of the uninitiated.

Today, those to whom this great treasure has been entrusted, namely, the priesthoods of the world, have forgotten that the Bibles are psychological dramas representing the consciousness of man; in their blind forgetfulness, they now teach their followers to worship its characters as men and women who actually lived in time and space.

When man sees the Bible as a great psychological drama, with all of its characters and actors as the personified qualities and attributes of his own consciousness, then – and then only – will the Bible reveal to him the light of its symbology.

This Impersonal principle of life which made all things is personified as God.

This Lord God, creator of heaven and earth, is discovered to be man's awareness of being.

If man were less bound by orthodoxy and more intuitively observant, he could not fail to notice in the reading of the Bibles that the awareness of being is revealed hundreds of times throughout this literature.

To name a few:

I AM hath sent me unto you.

—Exodus 3:14

Be still and know that I AM God.

—Psalm 46:10

I AM the Lord and there is no other God.
I am the LORD, and there is none else, there is no God beside Me.

—Isaiah 45:5

I am the LORD your God, and there is no other.
—Joel 2:27

I AM the shepherd.
I am the good shepherd: the good shepherd giveth His life for the sheep.
—John 10:11

I am the good shepherd, and know My sheep, and am known of Mine.
—John 10:14

I AM the door.
I am the door: by Me if any man enter in, he shall be saved, and shall go in and out, and find pasture.
—John 10:9

Verily, verily, I say unto you, I am the door of the sheep.
—John 10:7

I AM the resurrection and the life.
—John 11:25

I AM the way.
I am the way, and the truth, and the life; no one cometh to the Father but through Me.
—John 14:6

I AM the beginning and the end.
I am Alpha and Omega, the beginning and the end, the first and the last.
—Revelation 22:13

I am Alpha and Omega, the beginning and the ending, saith the Lord, Which is, and Which was, and Which is to come, the Almighty.
—Revelation 1:8

I AM; man's unconditioned awareness of being is revealed as Lord and Creator of every conditioned state of being.

If man would give up his belief in a God apart from himself, recognize his awareness of being to be God (this awareness fashions itself in the likeness and image of its conception of itself), he would transform his world from a barren waste to a fertile field of his own liking.

The day man does this he will know that he and his Father are one, but his Father is greater than he. He will know that his consciousness of being is one with that which he is conscious of being, but that his unconditioned consciousness of being is greater than his conditioned state or his conception of himself.

When man discovers his consciousness to be the impersonal power of expression, which power eternally personifies itself in his conceptions of himself, he will assume and appropriate that state of consciousness which he desires to express; in so doing he will become that state in expression.

"Ye shall decree a thing and it shall come to pass" can now be told in this manner: You shall become conscious of being or possessing a thing and you shall express or possess that which you are conscious of being.

The law of consciousness is the only law of expression.

"I AM the way." "I AM the resurrection."

Consciousness is the way as well as the power which resurrects and expresses all that man will ever be conscious of being.

Turn from the blindness of the uninitiated man who attempts to express and possess those qualities and things which he is not conscious of being and possessing; and be as the illumined mystic who decrees on the basis of this changeless law. Consciously claim yourself to be that which you seek; appropriate the consciousness of that which you see; and you too will know the status of the true mystic, as follows:

I became conscious of being it. I am still conscious of being it. And I shall continue to be conscious of being it until that which I am conscious of being is perfectly expressed.

Yes, I shall decree a thing and it shall come to pass.

CHAPTER 3

The Principle of Truth

Ye shall know the truth, and the truth shall make you free.
—John 8:32

The truth that sets man free is the knowledge that his consciousness is the resurrection and the life, that his consciousness both resurrects and makes alive all that he is conscious of being.

Apart from consciousness, there is neither resurrection nor life.

When man gives up his belief in a God apart from himself and begins to recognize his awareness of being to be God, as did Jesus and the prophets, he will transform his world with the realization,

I and My Father are one.
—John 10:30

but

My Father is greater than I.
—John 14:28

He will know that his consciousness is God and that which he is conscious of being is the Son bearing witness of God, the Father.

The conceiver and the conception are one, but the conceiver is greater than his conception. Before Abraham was, I AM. Yes, I was aware of being before I became aware of being man, and in that day when I shall cease to be conscious of being man I shall still be conscious of being.

The consciousness of being is not dependent upon being anything.

It preceded all conceptions of itself and shall be when all conceptions of itself shall cease to be. "I AM the beginning and the end". That is, all things or conceptions of myself begin and end in me, but I, the formless awareness, remain forever.

Jesus discovered this glorious truth and declared Himself to be one with God, not the God that man had fashioned, for He never recognized such a God.

Jesus found God to be His awareness of being and so told man that the Kingdom of God and Heaven were within [Luke 17:21,23].

When it is recorded that Jesus left the world and went to His Father — "He was received up into heaven" [Mark 16:19, Luke 24:51] — it is simply stating that He turned His attention from the world of the senses and rose in consciousness to that level which He desired to express.

There He remained until He became one with the consciousness to which He ascended. When He returned to the world of man, He could act with the positive assurance of that which He was conscious of being, a state of consciousness no one but Himself felt or knew that He possessed.

Man who is ignorant of this everlasting law of expression looks upon such happenings as miracles.

To rise in consciousness to the level of the thing desired and to remain there until such level becomes your nature is the way of all seeming miracles. "And I, if I be lifted up, I shall draw all men unto Me." "And I, if I be lifted up from the earth, will draw all men unto Me." [John 12:32]. If I be lifted up in consciousness to the naturalness of the thing desired, I shall draw the manifestation of that desire to me.

No man comes unto Me save the Father within Me draws him.
—John 6:44

and

I and My Father are one.

—John 10:30

My consciousness is the Father who draws the manifestation of life to me. The nature of the manifestation is determined by the state of consciousness in which I dwell. I am always drawing into my world that which I am conscious of being.

If you are dissatisfied with your present expression of life, then you must be born again [John 3:7]. Rebirth is the dropping of that level with which you are dissatisfied and rising to that level of consciousness which you desire to express and possess.

You cannot serve two masters [Matthew 6:24, Luke 16:13] or opposing states of consciousness at the same time.

Taking your attention from one state and placing it upon the other, you die to the one from which you have taken it and you live and express the one with which you are united.

Man cannot see how it would be possible to express that which he desires to be by so simple a law as acquiring the consciousness of the thing desired.

The reason for this lack of faith on the part of man is that he looks at the desired state through the consciousness of his present limitations. Therefore, he naturally sees it as impossible of accomplishment.

One of the first things man must realize is that it is impossible, in dealing with this spiritual law of consciousness, to put new wine into old bottles or new patches on old garments [Matthew 9:16,17; Mark 2:21,22; Luke 5:36-39].

That is, you cannot take any part of the present consciousness into the new state. For the state sought is complete in itself and needs no patching. Every level of consciousness automatically expresses itself.

To rise to the level of any state is to automatically become that state in expression. But, in order to rise to the level that you are not now expressing, you must completely drop the consciousness with which you are now identified.

Until your present consciousness is dropped, you will not be able to rise to another level.

Do not be dismayed. This letting go of your present identity is not as difficult as it might appear to be.

The invitation of the scriptures, "To be absent from the body and be present with the Lord" [2Corinthians 5:8, 1Corinthians 5:3, Colossians 2:5], is not given to a select few; it is a sweeping call to all mankind. The body from which you are invited to escape is your present conception of yourself with all of its limitations, while the Lord with whom you are to be present is your awareness of being.

To accomplish this seemingly impossible feat, you take your attention away from your problem and place it upon just being. You say silently but feelingly, "I AM". Do not condition this awareness but continue declaring quietly, "I AM – I AM". Simply feel that you are faceless and formless and continue doing so until you feel yourself floating.

"Floating" is a psychological state which completely denies the physical. Through practice in relaxation and willfully refusing to react to sensory impressions, it is possible to develop a state of consciousness of pure receptivity. It is a surprisingly easy accomplishment. In this state of complete detachment, a definite singleness of purposeful thought can be indelibly engraved upon your unmodified consciousness. This state of consciousness is necessary for true meditation.

This wonderful experience of rising and floating is the signal that you are absent from the body or problem and are now present with the Lord; in this expanded state you are not conscious of being anything but I AM – I AM; you are only conscious of being.

When this expansion of consciousness is attained, within this formless deep of yourself, give form to the new conception by claiming and feeling yourself to be that which you, before you entered into this state, desired to be. You will find that within this formless deep of yourself all things appear to be divinely possible. Anything that you sincerely feel yourself to be while in this expanded state becomes, in time, your natural expression.

And God said, "Let there be a firmament in the midst of the waters" [Genesis 1:6]. Yes, let there be a firmness or conviction in the midst of this expanded consciousness by knowing and feeling I AM that, the thing desired.

As you claim and feel yourself to be the thing desired, you are crystallizing this formless liquid light that you are into the image and likeness [Genesis 1:26] of that which you are conscious of being.

Now that the law of your being has been revealed to you, begin this day to change your world by revaluing yourself. Too long has man held to the belief that he is born of sorrow and must work out his salvation by the sweat of his brow. God is impersonal and no respecter of persons [Acts 10:34; Romans 2:11]. So long as man continues to walk in this belief of sorrow, so long will he walk. In a world of sorrow and confusion, for the world in its every detail is man's consciousness crystallized.

In the Book of Numbers it is recorded:

There were giants in the land and we were in our own sight as grasshoppers, and we were in their sight as grasshoppers.
—Numbers 13:33

Today is the day, the eternal now, when conditions in the world have attained the appearance of giants. The unemployed, the armies of the enemy, business competition etc. are the giants which make you feel yourself to be a helpless grasshopper. We are told we were first in our own sight helpless grasshoppers and because of this conception of ourselves were to the enemy helpless grasshoppers.

We can be to others only that which we are to ourselves.

Therefore, as we revalue ourselves and begin to feel ourselves to be the giant, a center of power, we automatically change our relationship to the giants, reducing these former monsters to their true place, making them appear to be the helpless grasshoppers.

Paul said of this principle, "It is to the Greeks *(or the so-called wise men of the world)* foolishness; and to the Jews *(or those who look for signs)* a stumbling block." "For the Jews require a sign, and the Greeks seek after wisdom; but we preach Christ crucified, unto the Jews a stumbling block, and unto the Greeks foolishness. But unto them which are called, both Jews and Greeks, Christ the power of God, and the wisdom of God. Because the foolishness of God is wiser than men;

and the weakness of God is stronger than men." 1Corinthians 1:22-25]. With the result that man continues to walk in darkness rather than awake to the realization:

I AM the light of the world.
—Matthew 5:14; John 8:12

Man has so long worshiped the images of his own making that at first he finds this revelation blasphemous, but the day man discovers and accepts this principle as the basis of his life, that day man slays his belief in a God apart from himself.

The story of Jesus' betrayal in the Garden of Gethsemane is the perfect illustration of man's discovery of this principle. We are told, the crowds armed with staves and lanterns sought Jesus in the dark of night.

As they inquired after the whereabouts of Jesus (salvation), the voice answered, "I AM"; whereupon the entire crowd fell to the ground. On regaining their composure, they again asked to be shown the hiding place of the savior and again the savior said:

I have told you that I AM, therefore if ye seek Me, let all else go.
—John 18:8

Man in the darkness of human ignorance sets out on his search for God, aided by the flickering light of human wisdom.

As it is revealed to man that his I AM or awareness of being is his savior, the shock is so great, he mentally falls to the ground, for every belief that he has ever entertained tumbles as he realizes that his consciousness is the one and only savior.

The knowledge that his I AM is God compels man to let all others go for he finds it impossible to serve two Gods. Man cannot accept his awareness of being as God and at the same time believe in another deity.

With this discovery, man's human ear or hearing (understanding) is cut off by the sword of faith (Peter) as his perfect disciplined hearing (understanding) is restored by (Jesus) the knowledge that I AM is Lord and Savior.

Before man can transform his world, he must first lay this foundation or understanding.

I AM the Lord [and there is none else].
—Isaiah 45:5

Man must know that his awareness of being is God.

Until this is firmly established so that no suggestion or argument of others can shake him, he will find himself returning to the slavery of his former belief.

If ye believe not that I AM He, ye shall die in your sins.
—John 8:24

Unless man discovers that his consciousness is the cause of every expression of his life, he will continue seeking the cause of his confusion in the world of effects, and so shall die in his fruitless search.

I AM the vine and ye are the branches.
—John 15:5

Consciousness is the vine and that which you are conscious of being is as branches that you feed and keep alive. Just as a branch has no life except it be rooted in the vine, likewise things have no life except you be conscious of them.

Just as a branch withers and dies if the sap of the vine ceases to flow towards it, so do things and qualities pass away if you take your attention from them; because your attention is the sap of life which sustains the expression of your life.

CHAPTER 4

Whom Seek Ye?

I have told you that I AM; if therefore ye seek Me, let these go their way.

—John 18:8

As soon then as He had said unto them, I AM, they went backward and fell to the ground.

—John 18:6

Today there is so much said about Masters, Elder Brothers, Adepts, and initiates that numberless truth seekers are being constantly misled by seeking these false lights.

For a price, most of these pseudo-teachers offer their students initiation into the mysteries, promising them guidance and direction. Man's weakness for leaders, as well as his worship of idols, makes him an easy prey of these schools and teachers.

Good will come to most of these enrolled students; they will discover after years of awaiting and sacrificing that they were following a mirage.

They will then become disillusioned in their schools and teachers, and this disappointment will be worth the effort and price they have paid for their fruitless search.

They will then turn from their worship of man and in so doing discover that which they are seeking is not to be found in another, for the Kingdom of Heaven is within [Luke 17:21].

This realization will be their first real initiation.

The lesson learned will be this: There is only one Master and this Master is God — the I AM within themselves.

> *I AM the Lord thy God who led thee out of the land of darkness; out of the house of bondage.*
> —Exodus 20:2, Deuteronomy 5:6

I AM — your awareness — is Lord and Master, and besides your awareness there is neither Lord nor Master.

You are Master of all that you will ever be aware of being.

You know that you are, do you not? Knowing that you are is the Lord and Master of that which you know that you are.

You could be completely isolated by man from that which you are conscious of being; yet you would, in spite of all human barriers, effortlessly draw to yourself all that you were conscious of being.

The man who is conscious of being poor does not need the assistance of anyone to express his poverty. The man who is conscious of being sick, though isolated in the most hermetically sealed germ-proof area in the world, would express sickness.

There is no barrier to God, for God is your awareness of being.

Regardless of what you are aware of being, you can and do express it without effort.

Stop looking for the Master to come; he is with you always.

> *I AM with you always, even unto the end of the world.*
> —Matthew 28:20

You will from time to time know yourself to be many things, but you need not be anything to know that you are.

You can, if you so desire, disentangle yourself from the body you wear; in so doing, you realize that you are a faceless, formless awareness and not dependent on the form you are in your expression.

You will know that you are; you will also discover that this "knowing that you are" is God, the Father, which preceded all that you ever knew yourself to be.

Before the world was, you were aware of being, and so you were saying "I AM", and I AM will be; after all that you know yourself to be shall cease to be.

There are no Ascended Masters. Banish this superstition.

You will forever rise from one level of consciousness (master) to another; in so doing, you manifest the ascended level, expressing this newly acquired consciousness.

Consciousness being Lord and Master, you are the Master Magician conjuring that which you are now conscious of being.

For God (consciousness) calleth those things which be not as though they were.
—Romans 4:17

Things that are not now seen will be seen the moment you become conscious of being that which is not now seen.

This rising from one level of consciousness to another is the only ascension that you will ever experience.

No man can lift you to the level you desire. The power to ascend is within yourself; it is your consciousness.

You appropriate the consciousness of the level you desire to express by claiming that you are now expressing such a level.

This is the ascension. It is limitless, for you will never exhaust your capacity to ascend.

Turn from the human superstition of ascension with its belief in masters, and find the only and everlasting master within yourself.

Far greater is he that is in you than he that is in the world.
—1 John 4:4

Believe this.

Do not continue in blindness, following after the mirage of masters. I assure you your search can end only in disappointment.

If you deny Me (your awareness of being), I shall deny you also.
—Matthew 10:33

Thou shalt have no other God beside ME.
—Isaiah 45:5; Joel 2:27

Be still and know that I AM God.
—Psalm 46:10

Come prove me and see if I will not open you the windows of Heaven and pour you out a blessing, that there shall not be room enough to receive it.
—Malachi 3:10

Do you believe that the I AM is able to do this?

Then claim ME to be that which you want to see poured out.

Claim yourself to be that which you want to be and that you shall be.

Not because of masters will I give it unto you, but because you have recognized ME (yourself) to be that, I will give it unto you, for I AM all things to all.

Jesus would not permit Himself to be called Good Master. He knew that there is but one good and one master. He knew this one to be His Father in Heaven, the awareness of being. "The Kingdom of God" (Good) and the Kingdom of Heaven are within you [Luke 17:21].

Your belief in masters is a confession of your slavery. Only slaves have masters.

Change your conception of yourself and you will, without the aid of masters or anyone else, automatically transform your world to conform to your changed conception of yourself.

You are told in the Book of Numbers that there was a time when men were in their own eyes as grasshoppers and because of this conception of themselves, they saw giants in the land. This is as true of man today as it was the day it was recorded. Man's conception of himself is so grasshopper-like, that he automatically makes the conditions round about him appear gigantic; in his blindness he cries out for masters to help him fight his giant problems.

Jesus tried to show man that salvation was within himself and warned him not to look for his savior in places or people.

If anyone should come saying look here or look there, believe him not, for the Kingdom of Heaven is within you.
—Luke 17:21

Jesus not only refused to permit Himself to be called Good Master, He warned his followers, "Salute no man along the highway," "and greet no man along the way" [Luke 10:4; 2Kings 4:29]. He made it clear that they should not recognize any authority or superior other than God, the Father.

Jesus established the identity of the Father as man's awareness of being. "I and My Father are one, but My Father is greater than I" [John 10:30, John 14:28]. I AM one with all that I am conscious of being. I AM greater than that which I am aware of being. The creator is ever greater than his creation.

"As Moses lifted up the serpent in the wilderness even so must the Son of Man be lifted up" [John 3:14]. The serpent symbolizes man's present conception of himself as a worm of the dust, living in the wilderness of human confusion. Just as Moses lifted himself from his worm-of-the-dust conception of himself to discover God to be his awareness of being, "I AM hath sent me" [Exodus 3:14], so must you be lifted up. The day you claim, as did Moses, "I AM that I AM" [Exodus 3:14], that day your claim will blossom in the wilderness.

Your awareness is the master magician who conjures all things by being that which he would conjure. This Lord and Master that you are can and does make all that you are conscious of being appear in your world.

"No man *(manifestation)* cometh unto Me save My Father draw him and I and My Father are one."

No man can come to Me, except the Father which hath sent Me draw him: and I will raise him up at the last day.
—John 6:44]

> *My Father, which gave them Me, is greater than all; and no man is able to pluck them out of My Father's hand. I and My Father are one.*
>
> —John 10:29, 30

You are constantly drawing to yourself that which you are conscious of being. Change your conception of yourself from that of the slave to that of Christ.

Don't be embarrassed to make this claim; only as you claim, "I AM Christ", will you do the works of Christ.

"The works I do ye shall do also, and greater works than these shall ye do, for I go unto my Father."

> *Truly, truly, I say to you, he who believes in Me, the works that I do, he will do also; and greater works than these he will do; because I go to the Father.*
>
> —John 14:12

> *He made Himself equal with God and found it not robbery to do the works of God.*
>
> —Philippians 2:6

Jesus knew that anyone who dared to claim himself to be Christ would automatically assume the capacities to express the works of his conception of Christ.

Jesus also knew that the exclusive use of this principle of expression was not given to Him alone.

He constantly referred to His Father in Heaven.

He stated that His works would not only be equaled but that they would be surpassed by that man who dared to conceive himself to be greater than He (Jesus) had conceived Himself to be.

Jesus, in stating that He and His Father were one but that His Father was greater than He, revealed His awareness (Father) to be one with that which He was aware of being.

He found Himself as Father or awareness to be greater than that which He as Jesus was aware of being.

You and your conception of yourself are one.

You are and always will be greater than any conception you will ever have of yourself.

Man fails to do the works of Jesus Christ because he attempts to accomplish them from his present level of consciousness.

You will never transcend your present accomplishments through sacrifice and struggle.

Your present level of consciousness will only be transcended as you drop the present state and rise to a higher level.

You rise to a higher level of consciousness by taking your attention away from your present limitations and placing it upon that which you desire to be. Do not attempt this in day-dreaming or wishful thinking, but in a positive manner.

Claim yourself to be the thing desired. I AM that; no sacrifice, no diet, no human tricks.

All that is asked of you is to accept your desire. If you dare claim it, you will express it.

Meditate on these:

I rejoice not in the sacrifices of men.
—(probably) Malachi 1:10

Not by might nor by power, but by my spirit.
—Zechariah 4:6

Ask and you shall receive.
—Matthew 7:7, Matthew 21:22, Mark 11:24, Luke 11:9, John 15:7, John 16:24

Come eat and drink without price.
—(probably) Isaiah 55:1

The works are finished. All that is required of you to let these qualities into expression is the claim – I AM that. Claim yourself to be that which you desire to be and that you shall be.

Expressions follow the impressions, they do not precede them. Proof that you are will follow the claim that you are, it will not precede it.

"Leave all and follow Me" [Matthew 8:22; 9:9; Luke 5:27] is a double invitation to you.

First, it invites you to turn completely away from all problems and, then, it calls upon you to continue walking in the claim that you are that which you desire to be.

Do not be a Lot's wife who looks back and becomes salted [Genesis 19] or preserved in the dead past.

Be a Lot who does not look back but who keeps his vision focused upon the promised land, the thing desired.

Do this and you will know that you have found the master, the Master Magician, making the unseen the seen through the command, "I AM THAT".

CHAPTER 5

Who Am I?

But whom say ye that I AM?

—Matt. 16:15

I AM the Lord; that is My name; and My glory will I not give to another.

—Isaiah 42:8

I AM the Lord, the God of all Flesh.

—Jeremiah 32:27

This I AM within you, the reader, this awareness, this consciousness of being, is the Lord, the God of all Flesh.

I AM is He that should come; stop looking for another. As long as you believe in a God apart from yourself, you will continue to transfer the power of your expression to your conceptions, forgetting that you are the conceiver.

The power conceiving and the thing conceived are one but the power to conceive is greater than the conception.

Jesus discovered this glorious truth when He declared:

I and My Father are one, but My Father is greater than I.

—John 10:30, John 14:28

The power conceiving itself to be man is greater than its conception. All conceptions are limitations of the conceiver.

Before Abraham was, I AM.

—John 8:58

Before the world was, I AM.

Consciousness precedes all manifestations and is the prop upon which all manifestation rests.

To remove the manifestations, all that is required of you, the conceiver, is to take your attention away from the conception. Instead of "Out of sight, out of mind", it really is "Out of mind, out of sight".

The manifestation will remain in sight only as long as it takes the force with which the conceiver – I AM – originally endowed it to spend itself. This applies to all creation from the infinitesimally small electron to the infinitely great universe.

Be still and know that I AM God.

—Psalm 46:10

Yes, this very I AM, your awareness of being, is God, the only God. I AM is the Lord – the God of all Flesh – all manifestation.

This presence, your unconditioned awareness, comprehends neither beginning nor ending; limitations exist only in the manifestation. When you realize that this awareness is your eternal self, you will know that before Abraham was, I AM.

Begin to understand why you were told:

Go thou and do likewise.

—Luke 10:37

Begin now to identify yourself with this presence, your awareness, as the only reality.

All manifestations but appear to be; you as man have no reality other than that which your eternal self, I AM, believes itself to be.

> *Whom do you say that I AM?*
> —Matthew 16:15, Mark 8:29, Luke 9:20

This is not a question asked two thousand years ago. It is the eternal question addressed to the manifestation by the conceiver.

It is your true self, your awareness of being, asking you, its present conception of itself, "Who do you believe your awareness to be?"

This answer can be defined only within yourself, regardless of the influence of another.

I AM *(your true self)* is not interested in man's opinion.

All its interest lies in your conviction of yourself.

What do you say of the I AM within you? Can you answer and say, "I AM Christ"?

Your answer or degree of understanding will determine the place you will occupy in life.

Do you say or believe yourself to be a man of a certain family race, nation, etc.? Do you honestly believe this of yourself?

Then life, your true self will cause these conceptions to appear in your world and you will live with them as though they are real.

> *I AM the door.*
> —John 10:9

> *I AM the way.*
> —John 14:6

> *I AM the resurrection and the life.*
> —John 11:25

> *No man (or manifestation) cometh unto My Father save by Me. I am the way, the truth, and the life: no man cometh unto the Father, but by Me.*
> —John 14:6

The I AM *(your consciousness)* is the only door through which anything can pass into your world.

Stop looking for signs. Signs follow; they do not precede. Begin to reverse the statement, "Seeing is believing", to "Believing is seeing". Start now to believe, not with the wavering confidence based on deceptive external evidence but with an undaunted confidence based on the immutable law that you can be that which you desire to be. You will find that you are not a victim of fate but a victim of faith *(your own)*.

Only through one door can that which you seek pass into the world of manifestation. "I AM the door". Your consciousness is the door, so you must become conscious of being and having that which you desire to be and to have. Any attempt to realize your desires in ways other than through the door of consciousness makes you a thief and a robber unto yourself.

Any expression that is not felt is unnatural. Before anything appears, God, I AM, feels itself to be the thing desired; and then the thing felt appears. It is resurrected; lifted out of the nothingness.

I AM wealthy, poor, healthy, sick, free, confined, were first of all impressions or conditions felt before they became visible expressions.

Your world is your consciousness objectified. Waste no time trying to change the outside; change the within or the impression; and the without or expression will take care of itself.

When the truth of this statement dawns upon you, you will know that you have found the lost word or the key to every door.

I AM *(your consciousness)* is the magical lost word which was made flesh in the likeness of that which you are conscious of being.

I AM He. Right now, I am overshadowing you, the reader, my living temple, with my presence, urging upon you a new expression. Your desires are my spoken words. My words are spirit and they are true and they shall not return unto me void but shall accomplish where unto they are sent.

> *So shall my word be that goeth forth out of my mouth: it shall not return unto me void, but it shall accomplish that which I please, and it shall prosper in the thing whereto I sent it.*
> —Isaiah 55:11

They are not something to be worked out.

They are garments that I, your faceless, formless self, wear. Behold! I, clothed in your desire, stand at the door (*your consciousness*) and knock. If you hear my voice and open unto me *(recognize me as your savior)*, I will come in unto you and sup with you and you with me.

> *Behold, I stand at the door, and knock: if any man hear my voice, and open the door, I will come in to him, and will sup with him, and he with me.*
> —Revelation 3:20

Just how my words, your desires, will be fulfilled, is not your concern. My words have a way ye know not of [John 4:32]. Their ways are past finding out [Romans 11:33].

All that is required of you is to believe. Believe your desires to be garments your savior wears. Your belief that you are now that which you desire to be is proof of your acceptance of life's gifts. You have opened the door for your Lord, clothed in your desire, to enter the moment you establish this belief.

> *When ye pray, believe that ye have received and it shall be so.*
> —Mark 11:24

> *All things are possible to him who believes.*
> —Mark 9:23

Make the impossible possible through your belief; and the impossible *(to others)* will embody itself in your world.

All men have had proof of the power of faith. The faith that moves mountains is faith in yourself.

No man has faith in God who lacks confidence in himself. Your faith in God is measured by your confidence in yourself. "I and My Father are one" [John 10:30]; man and his God are one, consciousness and manifestation are one.

And God said, "Let there be a firmament in the midst of the waters" [Genesis 1:6]. In the midst of all the doubts and changing opinions of others, let there be a conviction, a firmness of belief, and you shall see the dry land; your belief will appear.

The reward is to him that endureth unto the end: "But he that shall endure unto the end, the same shall be saved" [Matthew 24:13]. A conviction is not a conviction if it can be shaken. Your desire will be as clouds without rain unless you believe.

Your unconditioned awareness or I AM is the Virgin Mary who knew not a man [Luke 1:34], and yet, unaided by man, conceived and bore a son. Mary, the unconditioned consciousness, desired and then became conscious of being the conditioned state which she desired to express, and in a way unknown to others, became it. Go and do likewise; assume the consciousness of that which you desire to be and you, too, will give birth to your savior.

When the annunciation is made, when the urge or desire is upon you, believe it to be God's spoken word seeking embodiment through you. Go, tell no man of this holy thing that you have conceived. Lock your secret within you and magnify the Lord [Luke 1:46] — magnify or believe your desire to be your savior coming to be with you.

When this belief is so firmly established that you feel confident of results, your desire will embody itself. How it will be done, no man knows. I, your desire, have ways ye know not of [John 4:32]. My ways are past finding out [Romans 11:33]. Your desire can be likened to a seed, and seeds contain within themselves both the power and the plan of self-expression. Your consciousness is the soil. These seeds are successfully planted only if, after you have claimed yourself to be and to have that which you desire, you confidently await results without an anxious thought.

If I be lifted up in consciousness to the naturalness of my desire, I shall automatically draw the manifestation unto me.

Consciousness is the door through which life reveals itself. Consciousness is always objectifying itself.

To be conscious of being or possessing anything is to be or have that which you are conscious of being or possessing. Therefore, lift yourself to the consciousness of your desire and you will see it automatically out-picture itself.

To do this, you must deny your present identity. "Let him deny himself" [Mark 8:34]. You deny a thing by taking your attention away from it. To drop a thing, problem or ego from consciousness, you dwell upon God – God being I AM. Be still and know that I AM is God [Psalm 46:10].

Believe, feel that I AM; know that this knowing one within you, your awareness of being, is God.

Close your eyes and feel yourself to be faceless, formless and without figure. Approach this stillness as though it were the easiest thing in the world to accomplish. This attitude will assure your success.

When all thought of problem or self is dropped from consciousness because you are now absorbed or lost in the feeling of just being I AM, then begin in this formless state to feel yourself to be that which you desire to be, "I AM that I AM".

The moment you reach a certain degree of intensity so that you actually feel yourself to be a new conception, this new feeling or consciousness is established and in due time will personify itself in the world of form.

This new perception will express itself as naturally as you now express your present identity.

To express the qualities of a consciousness naturally, you must dwell or live within that consciousness. Appropriate it by becoming one with it. To feel a thing intensely, and then rest confidently that it is, makes the thing felt appear within your world.

"I shall stand upon my watch" [Habakkuk 2:1] "and see the salvation of the Lord" [2Chronicles 20:17]. I shall stand firmly upon my feeling, convinced that it is so, and see my desire appear.

A man can receive nothing (no thing) except it be given him from Heaven.
—John 3:27

Remember, heaven is your consciousness; the Kingdom of Heaven is within you.

This is why you are warned against calling any man Father; your consciousness is the Father of all that you are.

Again you are told, "Salute no man on the highway" [Luke 10:4; 2Kings 4:29]. See no man as an authority. Why should you ask man for permission to express when you realize that your world, in its every detail, originated within you and is sustained by you as the only conceptional center?

Your whole world may be likened to solidified space mirroring the beliefs and acceptances as projected by a formless, faceless presence, namely, I AM. Reduce the whole to its primordial substance and nothing would remain but you, a dimensionless presence, the conceiver.

The conceiver is a law apart. Conceptions under such law are not to be measured by past accomplishments or modified by present capacities for, without taking thought, the conception in a way unknown to man expresses itself.

Go within secretly and appropriate the new consciousness. Feel yourself to be it, and the former limitations shall pass away as completely and as easily as snow on a hot summer's day.

You will not even remember the former limitations; they were never part of this new consciousness.

This rebirth Jesus referred to when he said to Nicodemus, "Ye must be born again" [John 3:7], was nothing more than moving from one state of consciousness to another.

Whatsoever ye shall ask in My name, that will I do.
—John 14:13; similarly, John 15:16; John 16:23

This certainly does not mean to ask in words, pronouncing with the lips the sounds, God or Christ Jesus, for millions have asked in this manner without results.

To feel yourself to be a thing is to have asked for that thing in His name. I AM is the nameless presence. To feel yourself to be rich is to ask for wealth in His name.

I AM is unconditioned. It is neither rich nor poor, strong nor weak. In other words, in HIM there is neither Greek nor Jew, bond nor free, male nor female. These are all conceptions or limitations of the limitless, and therefore names of the nameless.

To feel yourself to be anything is to ask the nameless, I AM, to express that name or nature".

> *Ask whatsoever ye will in My name by appropriating the nature of the thing desired and I will give it unto you.*

CHAPTER 6

I Am He

For if ye believe not that I AM, ye shall die in your sins.
—John 8:24.

All things were made by Him; and without Him was not anything made that was made.
—John 1:3

This is a hard saying for those trained in the various systems of orthodox religion to accept, but there it stands.
All things, good, bad and indifferent, were made by God.

God made man (manifestation) in His own image; in the likeness of God made He him.
—Genesis 1:27

Apparently adding to this confusion, it is stated:

And God saw that his creation was good.
—Genesis 1:31

What are you going to do about this seeming anomaly? How is man going to correlate all things as good when that which he is taught denies this fact?

Either the understanding of God is erroneous or else there is something radically wrong with man's teaching.

To the pure all things are pure.
—Titus 1:15

This is another puzzling statement. All the good people, the pure people, the holy people, are the greatest prohibitionists. Couple the foregoing statement with this one, "There is no condemnation in Christ Jesus", and you get an impassable barrier to the self-appointed judges of the world.

There is therefore now no condemnation to them which are in Christ Jesus, who walk not after the flesh, but after the Spirit.
—Romans 8:1

Such statements mean nothing to the self-righteous judges blindly changing and destroying shadows. They continue in the firm belief that they are improving the world.

Man, not knowing that his world is his individual consciousness out-pictured, vainly strives to conform to the opinion of others rather than to conform to the one and only opinion existent, namely, his own judgment of himself.

When Jesus discovered His consciousness to be this wonderful law of self-government, He declared, "And now I sanctify Myself that they also might be sanctified through the truth."

And for their sakes I sanctify Myself, that they also might be sanctified through the truth.
—John 17:19

He knew that consciousness was the only reality, that things objectified were nothing more than different states of consciousness.

Jesus warned His followers to seek first the Kingdom of Heaven (that state of consciousness that would produce the thing desired) and all things would be added to them [Matthew 6:33].

He also stated,

I AM the truth.
—John 14:6

He knew that man's consciousness was the truth or cause of all that man saw his world to be. Jesus realized that the world was made in the likeness of man. He knew that man saw his world to be what it was because man was what he was.

In short, man's conception of himself determines that which he sees his world to be.

All things are made by God (consciousness) and without him there is nothing made that is made.
—John 1:3

Creation is judged good and very good because it is the perfect likeness of that consciousness which produced it.

To be conscious of being one thing and then see yourself expressing something other than that which you are conscious of being is a violation of the law of being; therefore, it would not be good. The law of being is never broken; man ever sees himself expressing that which he is conscious of being.

Be it good, bad or indifferent, it is nevertheless a perfect likeness of his conception of himself; it is good and very good.

Not only are all things made by God, all things are made of God. All are the offspring of God. God is one. Things or divisions are the projections of the one. God being one, He must command Himself to be the seeming other, for there is no other.

The absolute cannot contain something within itself that is not itself. If it did, then it would not be absolute, the only one.

Commands, to be effective, must be to oneself. "I AM that I AM" is the only effective command.

I AM the Lord and beside Me there is none else.
—Isaiah 45:5; Joel 2:27

You cannot command that which is not. As there is no other, you must command yourself to be that which you would have appear.

Let me clarify what I mean by effective command. You do not repeat like a parrot the statement, "I AM that I AM"; such vain repetition would be both stupid and fruitless.

It is not the words that make it effective; it is the consciousness of being the thing which makes it effective.

When you say, "I AM", you are declaring yourself to be. The word that in the statement, "I AM that I AM", indicates that which you would be. The second "I AM" in the quotation is the cry of victory.

This whole drama takes place inwardly with or without the use of words.

Be still and know that you are.

This stillness is attained by observing the observer.

Repeat quietly but with feeling, "I AM – I AM", until you have lost all consciousness of the world and know yourself just as being.

Awareness, the knowing that you are, is Almighty God — I AM.

After this is accomplished, define yourself as that which you desire to be by feeling yourself to be the thing desired: I AM *that*. This understanding that you are the thing desired will cause a thrill to course through your entire being. When the conviction is established and you really believe that you are that which you desired to be, then the second "I AM" is uttered as a cry of victory. This mystical revelation of Moses can be seen as three distinct steps: I AM; I AM free; I really AM!

It does not matter what the appearances round about you are like. All things make way for the coming of the Lord. I AM the Lord coming in the appearance of that which I am conscious of being. All the inhabitants of the earth cannot stay my coming or question my authority to be that which I AM conscious that I AM.

> *All the inhabitants of the earth are as nothing, and He doeth according to His will in the armies of Heaven and among all the inhabitants of the earth; and none can stay His hand, nor say unto Him, 'What doest Thou?'*
>
> —Daniel 4:35

"I AM the light of the world" [John 8:12], crystallizing into the form of my conception of myself.

Consciousness is the eternal light, which crystallizes only through the medium of your conception of yourself.

Change your conception of yourself and you will automatically change the world in which you live. Do not try to change people; they are only messengers telling you who you are. Revalue yourself and they will confirm the change.

Now you will realize why Jesus sanctified Himself instead of others [John 17:19], why to the pure all things are pure [Titus 1:15], why in Christ Jesus (the awakened consciousness) there is no condemnation [Romans 8:1].

Awake from the sleep of condemnation and prove the principle of life. Stop not only your judgment of others but your condemnation of yourself.

Hear the revelation of the enlightened:

I know and am persuaded by the Lord Christ Jesus that there is nothing unclean of itself, but to him that seeth anything to be unclean to him it is unclean.
—Romans 14:14

And again,

Happy is the man who condemneth himself not in that which he alloweth.

Happy is he that condemneth not himself in that thing which he alloweth.
—Romans 14:22

Stop asking yourself whether or not you are worthy or unworthy to claim yourself to be that which you desire to be. You will be condemned by the world only as long as you condemn yourself.

You do not need to work out anything. The works are finished. The principle by which all things are made and without which there is not anything made that is made is eternal. You are this principle.

Your awareness of being is this everlasting law. You have never expressed anything that you were not aware of being and you never will. Assume the consciousness of that which you desire to express. Claim it until it becomes a natural manifestation. Feel it and live within that feeling until you make it your nature.

Here is a simple formula. Take your attention from your present conception of yourself and place it on that ideal of yours, the ideal you had heretofore thought beyond your reach. Claim yourself to be your ideal, not as something that you will be in time, but as that which you are in the immediate present.

Do this, and your present world of limitations will disintegrate as your new claim rises like the phoenix from its ashes.

> *Be not afraid nor dismayed by reason of this great multitude; for the battle is not yours, but God's.*
> —2 Chronicles 20:15

You do not fight against your problem; your problem will only live as long as you are conscious of it. Take your attention away from your problem and the multitude of reasons why you cannot achieve your ideal. Concentrate your attention entirely upon the thing desired.

> *Leave all and follow me*
> —Matthew 8:22; 9:9; Luke 5:27

In the face of seemingly mountainous obstacles, claim your freedom. The consciousness of freedom is the Father of freedom. It has a way of expressing itself which no man knows.

> *Ye shall not need to fight in this battle. Set yourself, stand still, and see the salvation of the Lord with you*
> —2 Chronicles 20:17

"I AM the Lord." I AM (your consciousness) is the Lord. The consciousness that the thing is done, that the work is finished, is the Lord of any situation.

Listen carefully to the promise,

Ye shall not need to fight in this battle. Set yourself, stand still, and see the salvation of the Lord with you.
—2 Chronicles 20:17

With you!

That particular consciousness with which you are identified is the Lord of the agreement. He will without assistance establish the thing agreed upon on earth.

Can you, in the face of the army of reasons why a thing cannot be done, quietly enter into an agreement with the Lord that it is done?

Can you, now that you have found the Lord to be your awareness of being, become aware that the battle is won?

Can you, no matter how near and threatening the enemy seems to be, continue in your confidence, standing still, knowing that the victory is yours?

If you can, you will see the salvation of the Lord. Remember, the reward is to the one who endures [Matthew 24:13].

Stand still.
—Psalm 46:10

Standing still is the deep conviction that all is well; it is done. No matter what is heard or seen, you remain unmoved, conscious of being victorious in the end.

All things are made by such agreements, and without such an agreement, there is not anything made that is made [John 1:3].

I AM that I AM.
—Exodus 3:14

In Revelations, it is recorded that a new heaven and new earth shall appear [21:1].

John, shown this vision, was told to write, "It is done" [21:6].

Heaven is your consciousness, and earth its solidified state. Therefore, accept as did John – "It is done".

All that is required of you who seek a change is to rise to a level of that which you desire; without dwelling upon the manner of expression, record that it is done by feeling the naturalness of being it.

Here is an analogy that might help you to see this mystery.

Suppose you entered a motion-picture theatre just as the feature picture came to its end. All that you saw of the picture was the happy-ending. Because you wanted to see the entire story, you waited for it to unfold again. With the anti-climactic sequence, the hero is displayed as accused, surrounded by false evidence, and all that goes to wring tears from the audience. But you, secure in the knowledge of the ending, remain calm with the understanding that, regardless of the seeming direction of the picture, the end has already been defined.

In like manner, go to the end of that which you seek; witness the happy end of it by consciously feeling you express and possess that which you desire to express and possess; and you, through faith, already understanding the end, will have confidence born of this knowledge.

This knowledge will sustain you through the necessary interval of time that it takes the picture to unfold.

Ask no help of man. Feel "It is done" by consciously claiming yourself to be now that which as man you hope to be.

CHAPTER 7

Thy Will Be Done

Not My will, but Thine, be done.

—Luke 22:42

O My Father, if this cup may not pass away from Me, except I drink it, Thy will be done.

—Matthew 26:42

Nevertheless not what I will, but what Thou wilt.

—Mark 14:36

This resignation is not one of blind realization that "I can of Myself do nothing, the Father within Me, He doeth the work."

I can of Mine own Self do nothing; as I hear, I judge, and My judgment is just because I seek not Mine own will, but the will of the Father which hath sent Me.

—John 5:30

Believest thou not that I am in the Father, and the Father in Me? The words that I speak unto you I speak not of Myself; but the Father that dwelleth in Me, He doeth the works.

—John 14:10

When man wills, he attempts to make something which does not now exist appear in time and space.

Too often we are not aware of that which we are really doing. We unconsciously state that we do not possess the capacities to express. We predicate our desire upon the hope of acquiring the necessary capacities in future time. "I AM not, but I will be".

Man does not realize that consciousness is the Father which does the work, so he attempts to express that which he is not conscious of being.

Such struggles are doomed to failure; only the present expresses itself. Unless I am conscious of being that which I seek, I will not find it. God (your awareness) is the substance and fullness of all.

God's will is the recognition of that which *is*, not of that which *will be*.

Instead of seeing this saying as "Thine will be done", see it as "Thy will is done". The works are finished.

The principle by which all things are made visible is eternal.

"Eyes have not seen nor ears heard, neither hath it entered into the hearts of men, the things which God hath prepared for those who love the law"

> *Eye hath not seen nor ear heard, neither hath entered into the heart of man, the things which God hath prepared for them that love Him.*
> —1 Corinthians 2:9-10

When a sculptor looks at a formless piece of marble he sees, buried within its formless mass, his finished piece of art. The sculptor, instead of making his masterpiece, merely reveals it by removing that part of the marble which hides his conception.

The same applies to you. In your formless awareness lies buried all that you will ever conceive yourself to be.

The recognition of this truth will transform you from an unskilled laborer who tries to make it so to a great artist who recognizes it to be so.

Your claim that you are now that which you want to be will remove the veil of human darkness and reveal your claim perfectly; I AM that.

God's will was expressed in the words of the Widow, "It is well". Man's will would have been, "It will be well". To state, "I shall be well", is to say, "I am ill".

God, the Eternal Now, is not mocked by words or vain repetition.

God continually personifies that which is.

Thus, the resignation of Jesus (who made Himself equal with God) was turning from the recognition of lack (which the future indicates with "I shall be") to the recognition of supply by claiming, "I AM that; it is done; thank You, Father".

Now you will see the wisdom in the words of the prophet when he states:

Let the weak say, I AM strong.

—Joel 3:10.

Man in his blindness will not heed the prophet's advice; he continues to claim himself to be weak, poor, wretched and all the other undesirable expressions from which he is trying to free himself by ignorantly claiming that he will be free from these characteristics in the expectancy of the future.

Such thoughts thwart the one law that can ever free him.

There is only one door through which that which you seek can enter your world. "I AM the door" [John 10:9].

When you say, "I AM", you are declaring yourself to be, first person, present tense; there is no future.

To know that I AM is to be conscious of being. Consciousness is the only door. Unless you are conscious of being that which you seek, you seek in vain.

If you judge after appearances, you will continue to be enslaved by the evidence of your senses.

To break this hypnotic spell of the senses, you are told, "Go within and shut the door"

> *But thou, when thou prayest, enter into thy closet, and when thou hast shut thy door, pray to thy Father which is in secret; and thy Father which seeth in secret shall reward thee openly.*
> —Matthew 6:6

> *Enter thou into thy chambers, and shut thy doors about thee: hide thyself as it were for a little moment, until the indignation be overpast.*
> —Isaiah 26:20

> *And when thou art come in, thou shalt shut the door upon thee and upon thy sons.*
> —2 Kings 4:4

> *He went in therefore, and shut the door upon them twain, and prayed unto the Lord.*
> —2 Kings 4:33

The door of the senses must be tightly shut before your new claim can be honored.

Closing the door of the senses is not as difficult as it appears to be at first. It is done without effort.

It is impossible to serve two masters at the same time [Matthew 6:24, Luke 16:13].

The master man serves is that which he is conscious of being. I am Lord and Master of that which I am conscious of being.

It is no effort for me to conjure poverty if I am conscious of being poor.

My servant (poverty) is compelled to follow me (conscious of poverty) as long as I AM (the Lord) conscious of being poor.

Instead of fighting against the evidence of the senses, you claim yourself to be that which you desire to be.

As your attention is placed on this claim, the doors of the senses automatically close against your former master (that which you were conscious of being).

As you become lost in the feeling of being (that which you are now claiming to be true of yourself), the doors of the senses once more open, revealing your world to be the perfect expression of that which you are conscious of being.

Let us follow the example of Jesus who realized, as man, He could do nothing to change His present picture of lack.

He closed the door of His senses against His problem and went to His Father, the one to Whom all things are possible [Matthew 19:26; Mark 9:23; 10:27; 14:36; Luke 18:27; Acts 8:37].

Having denied the evidence of His senses, He claimed Himself to be all that, a moment before, His senses told him He was not.

Knowing that consciousness expresses its likeness on earth, He remained in the claimed consciousness until the doors (His senses) opened and confirmed the rulership of the Lord.

Remember, I AM is Lord of all. Never again use the will of man which claims, "I will be". Be as resigned as Jesus and claim, "I AM that".

CHAPTER 8

No Other God

I am the first, and I am the last; and beside Me is no God.
—Isaiah 44:6

I am the Lord thy God, which brought thee out of the land of Egypt, from the house of bondage. Thou shalt have none other gods before Me.
—Deut. 5:6,7

"Thou shalt have no other God beside Me." As long as man entertains a belief in a power apart from himself, so long will he rob himself of the being that he is.

Every belief in powers apart from himself, whether for good or evil, will become the mould of the graven image worshipped.

The beliefs in the potency of drugs to heal, diets to strengthen, moneys to secure, are the values or money changers that must be thrown out of the power [Matthew 21:12; Mark 11:15; Luke 19:45; John 2:14,15] he can then unfailingly manifest that quality.

This understanding throws out the money changers Temple.

Ye are the Temple of the Living God.
—1 Corinthians 3:16; 6:19

As you become lost in the feeling of being (that which you are now claiming to be true of yourself), the doors of the senses once more open, revealing your world to be the perfect expression of that which you are conscious of being.

Let us follow the example of Jesus who realized, as man, He could do nothing to change His present picture of lack.

He closed the door of His senses against His problem and went to His Father, the one to Whom all things are possible [Matthew 19:26; Mark 9:23; 10:27; 14:36; Luke 18:27; Acts 8:37].

Having denied the evidence of His senses, He claimed Himself to be all that, a moment before, His senses told him He was not.

Knowing that consciousness expresses its likeness on earth, He remained in the claimed consciousness until the doors (His senses) opened and confirmed the rulership of the Lord.

Remember, I AM is Lord of all. Never again use the will of man which claims, "I will be". Be as resigned as Jesus and claim, "I AM that".

CHAPTER 8

No Other God

I am the first, and I am the last; and beside Me is no God.

—Isaiah 44:6

I am the Lord thy God, which brought thee out of the land of Egypt, from the house of bondage. Thou shalt have none other gods before Me.

—Deut. 5:6,7

"Thou shalt have no other God beside Me." As long as man entertains a belief in a power apart from himself, so long will he rob himself of the being that he is.

Every belief in powers apart from himself, whether for good or evil, will become the mould of the graven image worshipped.

The beliefs in the potency of drugs to heal, diets to strengthen, moneys to secure, are the values or money changers that must be thrown out of the power [Matthew 21:12; Mark 11:15; Luke 19:45; John 2:14,15] he can then unfailingly manifest that quality.

This understanding throws out the money changers Temple.

Ye are the Temple of the Living God.

—1 Corinthians 3:16; 6:19

And what agreement hath the temple of God with idols? For ye are the temple of the living God. As God hath said, 'I will dwell in them, and walk in them; and I will be their God, and they shall be my people.'
—2 Corinthians 6:16

A temple made without hands.
It is written:

My house shall be called of all nations a house of prayer, but ye have made it a den of thieves.
—Matthew 21:13

...for Mine house shall be called an house of prayer for all people.
—Isaiah 56:7

The thieves who rob you are your own false beliefs. It is your belief in a thing, not the thing itself, that aids you. There is only one power: I AM He. Because of your belief in external things, you think power into them by transferring the power that you are to the external thing. Realize you yourself are the power you have mistakenly given to outer conditions.

The Bible compares the opinionated man to the camel who could not go through the needle's eye [Matthew 19:24; Mark 10:25; Luke 18:25]. The needle's eye referred to was a small gate in the walls of Jerusalem, which was so narrow that a camel could not go through it until relieved of its pack.

The rich man, that is the one burdened with false human concepts, cannot enter the Kingdom of Heaven until relieved of his burden any more than could the camel go through this small gate [Matthew 19:23].

Man feels so secure in his man-made laws, opinions, and beliefs that he invests them with an authority they do not possess.

Satisfied that his knowledge is all, he remains unaware that all outward appearances are but states of mind externalized.

When he realizes that the consciousness of a quality externalizes that quality without the aid of any other or many values and establishes the one true value, his own consciousness.

The Lord is in His holy temple.
—Habakkuk 2:20

Consciousness dwells within that which it is conscious of being. I AM is the Lord and man, his temple.

Knowing that consciousness objectifies itself, man must forgive all men for being that which they are. He must realize that all are expressing (without the aid of another) that which they are conscious of being.

Peter, the enlightened or disciplined man, knew that a change of consciousness would produce a change of expression. Instead of sympathizing with the beggars of life at the temple's gate, he declared:

Silver and gold have I none (for thee), but such as I have (the consciousness of freedom), give I unto thee
—Acts 3:6

Stir up the gift within you.

Wherefore I put thee in remembrance that thou stir up the gift of God, which is in thee.
—2 Timothy 1:6

Stop begging and claim yourself to be that which you decide to be. Do this and you too will jump from your crippled world into the world of freedom, singing praises to the Lord, I AM. "Far greater is He that is in you than he that is in the world."

Ye are of God, little children, and have overcome them: because greater is He that is in you, than he that is in the world.
—1 John 4:4

This is the cry of everyone who finds his awareness of being to be God.

Your recognition of this fact will automatically cleanse the temple, your consciousness, of the thieves and robbers, restoring to you that dominion over things, which you lost the moment you forgot the command:

Thou shalt have no other God beside ME.

CHAPTER 9

The Foundation Stone

Let every man take heed how he buildeth thereon. For other foundations can no man lay than that is laid, which is Jesus Christ. Now if man build upon this foundation gold, silver, precious stones, wood, hay, stubble; every man's work shall be made manifest; for the day shall declare it.
—1 Cor. 3:10-13

The foundation of all expression is consciousness. Try as man will, he cannot find a cause of manifestation other than his consciousness of being.

Man thinks he has found the cause of disease in germs, the cause of war in conflicting political ideologies and greed. All such discoveries of man, catalogued as the essence of Wisdom, are foolishness in the eyes of God.

There is only one power and this power is God (consciousness). It kills; it makes alive; it wounds; it heals; it does all things, good, bad or indifferent.

Man moves in a world that is nothing more or less than his consciousness objectified. Not knowing this, he wars against his reflections while he keeps alive the light and the images which project the reflections.

I AM the light of the world.
—John 8:12

I AM (consciousness) is the light.

That which I am conscious of being (my conception of myself) – such as "I am rich", "I am healthy", "I am free" – are the images.

The world is the mirror magnifying all that I AM conscious of being.

Stop trying to change the world since it is only the mirror. Man's attempt to change the world by force is as fruitless as breaking a mirror in the hope of changing his face. Leave the mirror and change your face. Leave the world alone and change your conceptions of yourself. The reflection then will be satisfactory.

Freedom or imprisonment, satisfaction or frustration, can only be differentiated by the consciousness of being.

Regardless of your problem, its duration or its magnitude, careful attention to these instructions will in an amazingly short time eliminate even the memory of the problem.

Ask yourself this question: "How would I feel if I were free?" The very moment you sincerely ask this question, the answer comes.

No man can tell another the satisfaction of his desire fulfilled. It remains for each within himself to experience the feeling and joy of this automatic change of consciousness.

The feeling or thrill that comes to one in response to his self-questioning is the Father state of consciousness or Foundation Stone upon which the conscious change is built.

Just how this feeling will embody itself no one knows, but it will. The Father (consciousness) has ways that no man knows [Romans 11:33]; it is the unalterable law. All things express their nature. As you wear a feeling, it becomes your nature.

It might take a moment or a year – it is entirely dependent upon the degree of conviction. As doubts vanish and you can feel "I AM this", you begin to develop the fruit or the nature of the thing you are feeling yourself to be.

When a person buys a new hat or pair of shoes, he thinks everyone knows that they are new. He feels unnatural with his newly acquired apparel until it becomes a part of him. The same applies to the wearing of the new states of consciousness.

When you ask yourself the question, "How would I feel if my desire were at this moment realized?", the automatic reply, until it is properly conditioned by time and use, is actually disturbing. The period of adjustment to realize this potential of consciousness is comparable to the newness of the wearing apparel.

Not knowing that consciousness is ever outpicturing itself in conditions round about you, like Lot's wife, you continually look back upon your problem and again become hypnotized by its seeming naturalness [Genesis 19].

Heed the words of Jesus (salvation):

Leave all and follow Me.
—Matthew 4:19 [Matthew 8:22; Matthew 16:24; Matthew 19:21; Mark 1:17; Mark 8:34; Mark 10:21; Luke 9:23; Luke 18:22

Let the dead bury the dead.
—Matthew 8:22; Luke 9:60

Your problem might have you so hypnotized by its seeming reality and naturalness that you find it difficult to wear the new feeling or consciousness of your savior. You must assume this garment if you would have results.

The stone (consciousness) which the builders rejected (would not wear) is the chief cornerstone, and other foundations no man can lay.

CHAPTER 10

To Him That Hath

Take heed therefore how ye hear; for whosoever hath, to him shall be given; and whosoever hath not, from him shall be taken even that which he seemeth to have.

—Luke 8:18

The Bible, which is the greatest psychological book ever written, warns man to be aware of what he hears; then follows this warning with the statement, "To him that hath it shall be given and to him that hath not it shall be taken away".

Though many look upon this statement as one of the most cruel and unjust of the sayings attributed to Jesus, it still remains a just and merciful law based upon life's changeless principle of expression.

Man's ignorance of the working of the law does not excuse him nor save him from the results.

Law is impersonal and therefore no respecter of persons [Acts 10:34; Romans 2:11].

Man is warned to be selective in that which he hears and accepts as true. Everything that man accepts as true leaves an impression on his consciousness and must in time be defined as proof or disproof.

Perceptive hearing is the perfect medium through which man registers impressions. A man must discipline himself to hear only that which he wants to hear, regardless of rumors or the evidence of his senses to the contrary. As he conditions his perceptive hearing, he will react only to those impressions which he has decided upon. This law never fails.

Fully conditioned, man becomes incapable of hearing other than that which contributes to his desire.

God, as you have discovered, is that unconditioned awareness which gives to you all that you are aware of being. To be aware of being or having anything is to be or have that which you are aware of being. Upon this changeless principle all things rest. It is impossible for anything to be other than that which it is aware of being.

"To him that hath (that which he is aware of being) it shall be given". Good, bad or indifferent – it does not matter – man receives multiplied a hundredfold that which he is aware of being. In keeping with this changeless law —"To him that hath not, it shall be taken from him and added to the one that hath"— the rich get richer and the poor get poorer. You can only magnify that which you are conscious of being.

All things gravitate to that consciousness with which they are in tune. Likewise, all things disentangle themselves from that consciousness with which they are out of tune.

Divide the wealth of the world equally among all men and in a short time, this equal division will be as originally disproportioned. Wealth will find its way back into the pockets of those from whom it was taken.

Instead of joining the chorus of the have-nots, who insist on destroying those who have, recognize this changeless law of expression. Consciously define yourself as that which you desire. Once defined, your conscious claim established, continue in this confidence until the reward is received. As surely as the day follows the night, any attribute, consciously claimed, will manifest itself.

Thus, that which to the sleeping orthodox world is a cruel and unjust law becomes to the enlightened one of the most merciful and just statements of truth.

I am come not to destroy but to fulfill.
—Matthew 5:17

Nothing is actually destroyed. Any seeming destruction is a result of a change in consciousness. Consciousness ever fills full the state in which it dwells. The state from which consciousness is detached seems to those not familiar with this law to be destructive. However, this is only preparatory to a new state of consciousness.

Claim yourself to be that which you want filled full.

Nothing is destroyed. All is fulfilled.
To him that hath it shall be given.

CHAPTER 11

Christmas

Behold, a virgin shall be with child and shall bring forth a Son, and they shall call His name Emmanuel, which being interpreted is God with us.

—Matthew 1:23

One of the most controversial statements in the New Testament concerns the virgin conception and subsequent birth of Jesus, a conception in which man had no part. It is recorded that a Virgin conceived a Son without the aid of man, then secretly and without effort gave birth to her conception. This is the foundation upon which all Christendom rests.

The Christian world is asked to believe this story, for man must believe the unbelievable to fully express the greatness that he is.

Scientifically, man might be inclined to discard the whole Bible as untrue because his reason will not permit him to believe that the virgin birth is physiologically possible; but the Bible is a message of the soul and must be interpreted psychologically if man is to discover its true symbology.

Man must see this story as a psychological drama rather than a statement of physical fact. In so doing, he will discover the Bible to be based on a law which, if self-applied, will result in a manifested expression transcending his wildest dreams of accomplishment. To apply this law of self-expression, man must be schooled in the belief and disciplined to stand upon the platform that "all things are possible to God" [Matthew 19:26; Mark 9:23; 10:27; 14:36; Luke 18:27; Acts 8:37].

The outstanding dramatic dates of the New Testament, namely, the birth, death and resurrection of Jesus, were timed and dated to coincide with certain astronomical phenomena. The mystics who recorded this story noticed that at certain seasons of the year beneficial changes on earth coincided with astronomical changes above. In writing this psychological drama, they have personified the story of the soul as the biography of man.

Using these cosmic changes, they have marked the Birth and Resurrection of Jesus to convey that the same beneficial changes take place psychologically in the consciousness of man as he follows the law.

Even to those who fail to understand it, the story of Christmas is one of the most beautiful stories ever told. When unfolded in the light of its mystic symbology, it is revealed as the true birth of every manifestation in the world.

This virgin birth is recorded as having taken place on December 25th or, as certain secret societies celebrate it, on Christmas Eve, at midnight of December 24th.

Mystics established this date to mark the birth of Jesus because it was in keeping with the great earthly benefits this astronomical change signifies.

The astronomical observations which prompted the authors of this drama to use these dates were all made in the northern hemisphere; so from an astronomical point of view, the reverse would be true if seen from the southern latitudes.

However, this story was recorded in the north and therefore was based on northern observation.

Man very early discovered that the sun played a most important part in his life, that without the sun, physical life as he knew it could not be. So these most important dates in the story of the life of Jesus are based upon the position of the sun as seen from the earth in the northern latitudes.

After the sun reaches its highest point in the heavens in June, it gradually falls southward, taking with it the life of the plant world so that by December almost all of nature has been stilled. Should the sun continue to fall southward, all nature would be stilled unto death.

However, on December 25th, the sun begins its great move northward, bringing with it the promise of salvation and life anew for the world. Each day, as the sun rises higher in the heavens, man gains confidence in being saved from death by cold and starvation, for he knows that as it moves northward and crosses the equator all nature will rise again, will be resurrected from its long winter sleep.

Our day is measured from midnight to midnight, and, since the visible day begins in the east and ends in the west, the ancients said the day was born of that constellation which occupied the eastern horizon at midnight. On Christmas Eve, or midnight of December 24th, the constellation Virgo is rising on the eastern horizon.

So it is recorded that this Son and Savior of the world was born of a virgin.

It is also recorded that this virgin mother was traveling through the night, that she stopped at an inn and was given the only available room among the animals and there in a manger, where the animals fed, the shepherds found the Holy Child.

The animals with whom the Holy Virgin was lodged are the holy animals of the zodiac. There in that constantly moving circle of astronomical animals stands the Holy Mother, Virgo, and there you will see her every midnight of December 24th, standing on the eastern horizon as the sun and savior of the world starts his journey northward.

Psychologically, this birth takes place in man on that day when man discovers his consciousness to be the sun and savior of his world. When man knows the significance of this mystical statement, "I am the light of the world" [Matthew 5:14; John 8:12], he will realize that his I AM, or consciousness, is the sun of his life, which sun radiates images upon the screen of space. These images are in the likeness of that which he, as man, is conscious of being. Thus qualities and attributes which appear to move upon the screen of his world are really projections of this light from within himself.

The numberless unrealized hopes and ambitions of man are the seeds which are buried within the consciousness or virgin womb of man. There they remain like the seeds of earth, held in the frozen waste of winter, waiting for the sun to move northward or for man to return to the knowledge of who he is. In returning he moves northward through recognition of his true self by claiming "I AM the light of the world".

When man discovers his consciousness or I AM to be God, the savior of his world, he will be as the sun in its northern passage.

All hidden urges and ambitions will then be warmed and stimulated into birth by this knowledge of his true self. He will claim that he is that which heretofore he hoped to be. Without the aid of any man, he will define himself as that which he desires to express.

He will discover that his I AM is the virgin conceiving without the aid of man, that all conceptions of himself, when felt, and fixed in consciousness, will be embodied easily as living realities in his world.

Man will one day realize that this whole drama takes place in his consciousness, that his unconditioned consciousness or I AM is the Virgin Mary desiring to express, that through this law of self-expression he defines himself as that which he desires to express, and that without the help or cooperation of anyone he will express that which he has consciously claimed and defined himself as being.

He will then understand why Christmas is fixed on December 25th, while Easter is a movable date; why upon the virgin conception the whole of Christendom rests; that his consciousness is the virgin womb or bride of the Lord receiving impressions as self-impregnations and then, without assistance, embodying these impressions as the expressions of his life.

CHAPTER 12

Crucifixion & Resurrection

I AM the Resurrection and the Life; he that believeth in Me, though he were dead, yet shall he live.
—John 11:25

The mystery of the crucifixion and the resurrection is so interwoven that, to be fully understood, the two must be explained together for one determines the other. This mystery is symbolized on earth in the rituals of Good Friday and Easter. You have observed that the anniversary of this cosmic event, announced every year by the church, is not a fixed date as are other anniversaries marking births and deaths, but that this day changes from year to year, falling anywhere from the 22nd day of March to the 25th day of April.

The day of resurrection is determined in this manner. The first Sunday after the full moon in Aries is celebrated as Easter. Aries begins on the 21st day of March and ends approximately on the 19th day of April. The sun's entry into Aries marks the beginning of Spring. The moon in its monthly transit around the earth will form sometime between March 21st and April 25th an opposition to the sun, which opposition is called a full moon. The first Sunday after this phenomenon of the heavens occurs is celebrated as Easter; the Friday preceding this day is observed as Good Friday.

This movable date should tell the observant one to look for some interpretation other than the one commonly accepted. These days do not mark the anniversaries of the death and resurrection of an individual who lived on earth.

Seen from the earth, the sun in its northern passage appears at the Spring season of the year to cross the imaginary line man calls the equator. So it is said by the mystic to be crossified or crucified that man might live. It is significant that soon after this event takes place, all nature begins to arise or resurrect itself from its long Winter's sleep. Therefore, it may be concluded that this disturbance of nature, at this season of the year, is due directly to this crossing. Thus, it is believed that the sun must shed its blood on the Passover.

If these days marked the death and resurrection of a man, they would be fixed so that they would fall on the same date every year as all other historical events are fixed, but obviously this is not the case.

These dates were not intended to mark the anniversaries of the death and resurrection of Jesus, the man. The scriptures are psychological dramas and will reveal their meaning only as they are interpreted psychologically. These dates are adjusted to coincide with the cosmic change which occurs at this time of the year, marking the death of the old year and the beginning or resurrecting of the new year or Spring. These dates do symbolize the death and resurrection of the Lord; but this Lord is not a man; it is your awareness of being.

It is recorded that He gave His life that you might live, "I AM come that you might have life and that you might have it more abundantly" [John 10:10]. Consciousness slays itself by detaching itself from that which it is conscious of being so that it may live to that which it desires to be.

Spring is the time of year when the millions of seeds, which all Winter lay buried in the ground, suddenly spring into visibility that man might live; and, because the mystical drama of the crucifixion and resurrection is in the nature of this yearly change, it is celebrated at this Spring season of the year; but, actually, it is taking place every moment of time.

The being who is crucified is your awareness of being. The cross is your conception of yourself. The resurrection is the lifting into visibility of this conception of yourself.

Far from being a day of mourning, Good Friday should be a day of rejoicing, for there can be no resurrection or expression unless there is first a crucifixion or impression.

The thing to be resurrected in your case is that which you desire to be. To do this, you must feel yourself to be the thing desired. You must feel "I AM the resurrection and the life of the desire".

I AM (your awareness of being) is the power resurrecting and making alive that which in your awareness you desire to be.

"Two shall agree on touching anything and I shall establish it on earth"

> *Again I say unto you, That if two of you shall agree on earth as touching any thing that they shall ask, it shall be done for them of my Father which is in heaven.*
> —Matthew 18:19

The two agreeing are you (your awareness – the consciousness desiring) and the thing desired. When this agreement is attained, the crucifixion is completed; two have crossed or crossified each other.

I AM and THAT – consciousness and that which you are conscious of being – have joined and are one; I AM now nailed or fixed in the belief that I AM this fusion.

Jesus or I AM is nailed upon the cross of that. The nail that binds you upon the cross is the nail of feeling.

The mystical union is now consummated and the result will be the birth of a child or the resurrection of a son bearing witness of his Father.

Consciousness is united to that which it is conscious of being. The world of expression is the child confirming this union.

The day you cease to be conscious of being that which you are now conscious of being, that day your child or expression shall die and return to the bosom of his father, the faceless, formless awareness.

All expressions are the results of such mystical unions.

So the priests are correct when they say that true marriages are made in heaven and can only be dissolved in heaven.

But let me clarify this statement by telling you that heaven is not a locality; it is a state of consciousness.

The Kingdom of Heaven is within you.
—Luke 17:21

In heaven (consciousness) God is touched by that which he is aware of being. "Who has touched me? For I perceive virtue has gone out of me."

'Who touched me?' And Jesus said, 'Somebody hath touched me: for I perceive that virtue is gone out of me'.
—Luke 8:45,46; Mark 5:30

The moment this touching (feeling) takes place, there is an offspring or going-out-of-me into visibility taking place.

The day man feels "I AM free", "I AM wealthy", "I AM strong", God (I AM) is touched or crucified by these qualities or virtues.

The results of such touching or crucifying will be seen in the birth or resurrection of the qualities felt, for man must have visible confirmation of all that he is conscious of being.

Now you will know why man or manifestation is always made in the image of God. Your awareness imag[in]es and outpictures all that you are aware of being.

I AM the Lord and besides me there is no God.
—Isaiah 45:5,6

I AM the Resurrection and the Life.
—John 11:25

You shall become fixed in the belief that you are that which you desire to be. Before you have any visible proof that you are, you will, from the deep conviction which you have felt fixed within you, know that you are; and so, without waiting for the confirmation of your senses, you will cry, "It is finished" [John 19:30].

Then, with a faith born of the knowledge of this changeless law, you will be as one dead and entombed; you will be still and unmoved in your conviction and confident that you will resurrect the qualities that you have fixed and are feeling within you.

CHAPTER 13

The I'm-Pressions

And as we have borne the image of the earthly, we shall also bear the image of the heavenly.

—1 Cor. 15:49

Your consciousness or your I AM is the unlimited potential upon which impressions are made. I'm-pressions are defined states pressed upon your I AM. Your consciousness or your I AM can be likened to a sensitive film. In the virgin state, it is potentially unlimited.

You can impress or record a message of love or a hymn of hate, a wonderful symphony or discordant jazz. It does not matter what the nature of the impression might be; your I AM will, without a murmur, willingly receive and sustain all impressions.

Your consciousness is the one referred to in Isaiah 53:3-7:

He is despised and rejected of men; a man of sorrows, and acquainted with grief: and we hid as it were our faces from Him, He was despised, and we esteemed Him not.

Surely He hath borne our grieves, and carried our sorrows: yet we did esteem Him stricken, smitten of God, and afflicted.

But He was wounded for our transgressions, He was bruised for our iniquities: the chastisement of our peace was upon him; and with his stripes we are healed.

All we like sheep have gone astray; we have turned every one to his own way; and the Lord hath laid on Him the iniquity of us all.

*He was oppressed, and He was afflicted,
yet He opened not his mouth:
He is brought as a lamb to the slaughter
and as a sheep before her shearers is dumb,
so He openeth not His mouth.*

Your unconditioned consciousness is impersonal; it is no respecter of persons.
—Acts 10:34; Romans 2:11

Without thought or effort, it automatically expresses every impression that is registered upon it. It does not object to any impression that is placed upon it for; although it is capable of receiving and expressing any and all defined states, it remains forever an immaculate and an unlimited potential.

Your I AM is the foundation upon which the defined state or conception of yourself rests; but it is not defined by, nor is it dependent on, such defined states for its being.

Your I AM neither expands nor contracts; nothing alters or adds to it. Before any defined state was, IT is. When all states cease to be, IT is. All defined states or conceptions of yourself are but ephemeral expressions of your eternal being.

To be impressed is to be I'm-pressed (I AM pressed – first person – present tense). All expressions are the result of I'm-pressions. Only as you claim yourself to be that which you desire to be will you express such desires.

Let all desires become impressions of qualities that are, not of qualities that will be. I'm (your awareness) is God, and God is the fullness of all, the Eternal NOW, I AM.

Take no thought of tomorrow; tomorrow's expressions are determined by today's impressions.

Now is the accepted time.

—2 Cor. 6:2, Isa. 49:8

The Kingdom of Heaven is at hand.

—Matthew 4:17

Jesus (salvation) said:

I am with you always.

—Matthew 28:20

Your awareness is the savior that is with you always; but, if you deny Him, He will deny you also [Matthew 10:33; Luke 12:9]. You deny Him by claiming that He will appear, as millions today are claiming that salvation is to come; this is the equivalent of saying, "We are not saved".

You must stop looking for your savior to appear and begin claiming that you are already saved, and the signs of your claims will follow.

When the widow was asked what she had in her house, there was recognition of substance; her claim was a few drops of oil [Kings 4:1-6]. A few drops will become a gusher if properly claimed. Your awareness magnifies all consciousness.

To claim that I shall have oil (joy) is to confess that I have empty measures. Such impressions of lack produce lack.

God, your awareness, is no respecter of persons [Acts 10:34; Romans 2:11]. Purely impersonal, God, this awareness of all existence, receives impressions, qualities and attributes defining consciousness — namely, your impressions.

Your every desire should be determined by need. Needs, whether seeming or real, will automatically be fulfilled when they are welcomed with sufficient intensity of purpose as defined desires.

Knowing that your awareness is God, you should look upon each desire as the spoken word of God, telling you that which is.

Cease ye from man, whose breath is in his nostrils: for wherein is he to be accounted of?

—Isaiah 2:22

We are ever that which is defined by our awareness. Never claim, "I shall be that". Let all claims from now on be, "I AM that I AM". Before we ask, we are answered. The solution of any problem associated with desire is obvious. Every problem automatically produces the desire of solution.

Man is schooled in the belief that his desires are things against which he must struggle. In his ignorance, he denies his savior who is constantly knocking at the door of consciousness to be let in (I AM the door).

Would not your desire, if realized, save you from your problem?

To let your savior in is the easiest thing in the world. Things must be, to be let in.

You are conscious of a desire; the desire is something you are aware of now. Your desire, though invisible, must be affirmed by you to be something that is real.

> *God calleth those things which be not (are not seen) as though they were.*
> —Romans 4:17

Claiming I AM the thing desired, I let the savior in.

> *Behold, I stand at the door, and knock: if any man hear My voice, and open the door, I will come in to him, and will sup with him, and he with Me.*
> —Revelation 3:20

Every desire is the savior's knock at the door.

This knock every man hears.

Man opens the door when he claims, "I AM He". See to it that you let your savior in.

Let the thing desired press itself upon you until you are I'm-pressed with nowness of your savior; then you utter the cry of victory:

> *It is finished.*
> —John 19:30

CHAPTER 14

Circumcision

In whom also ye are circumcised with the circumcision made without hands; in putting off the body of the sins of the flesh by circumcision of Christ.

—Col. 2:11

Circumcision is the operation which removes the veil that hides the head of creation. The physical act has nothing to do with the spiritual act.

The whole world could be physically circumcised and yet remain unclean and blind leaders of the blind.

The spiritually circumcised have had the veil of darkness removed and know themselves to be Christ, the light of the world.

Let me now perform the spiritual operation on you, the reader.

This act is performed on the eighth day after birth, not because this day has any special significance or in any way differs from other days, but it is performed on this eighth day because eight is the figure which has neither beginning nor end.

Furthermore, the ancients symbolized the eighth numeral or letter as an enclosure or veil within and behind which lay buried the mystery of creation.

Thus, the secret of the operation on the eighth day is in keeping with the nature of the act, which act is to reveal the eternal head of creation, that changeless something in which all things begin and end and yet which remains its eternal self when all things cease to be.

This mysterious something is your awareness of being. At this moment you are aware of being, but you are also aware of being someone. This someone is the veil that hides the being you really are.

You are first conscious of being, then you are conscious of being man. After the veil of man is placed upon your faceless self, you become conscious of being a member of a certain race, nation, family, creed etc.

The veil to be lifted in spiritual circumcision is the veil of man. But before this can be done, you must cut away the adhesions of race, nation, family and so on.

> *In Christ there is neither Greek nor Jew, bond nor free, male nor female.*
>
> *...a renewal in which there is no distinction between Greek and Jew, circumcised and uncircumcised, barbarian, Scythian, slave and freeman, but Christ is all, and in all.*
> —Colossians 3:11
>
> *You must leave father, mother, brother and follow me.*
>
> *If anyone comes to Me, and does not hate his own father and mother and wife and children and brothers and sisters, yes, and even his own life, he cannot be My disciple.*
> —Luke 14:26

To accomplish this you stop identifying yourself with these divisions by becoming indifferent to such claims. Indifference is the knife that severs. Feeling is the tie that binds.

When you can look upon man as one grand brotherhood without distinction of race or creed, then you will know that you have severed these adhesions.

With these ties cut, all that now separates you from your true being is your belief that you are man.

To remove this last veil, you drop your conception of yourself as man by knowing yourself just to be.

CHAPTER 14

Circumcision

In whom also ye are circumcised with the circumcision made without hands; in putting off the body of the sins of the flesh by circumcision of Christ.

—Col. 2:11

Circumcision is the operation which removes the veil that hides the head of creation. The physical act has nothing to do with the spiritual act.

The whole world could be physically circumcised and yet remain unclean and blind leaders of the blind.

The spiritually circumcised have had the veil of darkness removed and know themselves to be Christ, the light of the world.

Let me now perform the spiritual operation on you, the reader.

This act is performed on the eighth day after birth, not because this day has any special significance or in any way differs from other days, but it is performed on this eighth day because eight is the figure which has neither beginning nor end.

Furthermore, the ancients symbolized the eighth numeral or letter as an enclosure or veil within and behind which lay buried the mystery of creation.

Thus, the secret of the operation on the eighth day is in keeping with the nature of the act, which act is to reveal the eternal head of creation, that changeless something in which all things begin and end and yet which remains its eternal self when all things cease to be.

This mysterious something is your awareness of being. At this moment you are aware of being, but you are also aware of being someone. This someone is the veil that hides the being you really are.

You are first conscious of being, then you are conscious of being man. After the veil of man is placed upon your faceless self, you become conscious of being a member of a certain race, nation, family, creed etc.

The veil to be lifted in spiritual circumcision is the veil of man. But before this can be done, you must cut away the adhesions of race, nation, family and so on.

> *In Christ there is neither Greek nor Jew, bond nor free, male nor female.*
>
> *...a renewal in which there is no distinction between Greek and Jew, circumcised and uncircumcised, barbarian, Scythian, slave and freeman, but Christ is all, and in all.*
> —Colossians 3:11
>
> *You must leave father, mother, brother and follow me.*
>
> *If anyone comes to Me, and does not hate his own father and mother and wife and children and brothers and sisters, yes, and even his own life, he cannot be My disciple.*
> —Luke 14:26

To accomplish this you stop identifying yourself with these divisions by becoming indifferent to such claims. Indifference is the knife that severs. Feeling is the tie that binds.

When you can look upon man as one grand brotherhood without distinction of race or creed, then you will know that you have severed these adhesions.

With these ties cut, all that now separates you from your true being is your belief that you are man.

To remove this last veil, you drop your conception of yourself as man by knowing yourself just to be.

Instead of the consciousness of "I AM man", let there be just "I AM" – faceless, formless, and without figure.

You are spiritually circumcised when the consciousness of man is dropped and your unconditioned awareness of being is revealed to you as the everlasting head of creation, a formless, faceless all-knowing presence.

Then, unveiled and awake, you will declare and know that – I AM is God and beside me, this awareness, there is no God.

This mystery is told symbolically in the Bible story of Jesus washing the feet of his disciples. It is recorded that Jesus laid aside his garments and took a towel and girded himself. Then, after washing his disciples' feet, he wiped them with the towel wherewith he was girded. Peter protested the washing of his feet and was told that unless his feet were washed he would have no part of Jesus. Peter on hearing this replied, "Lord, not my feet only, but also my hands and my head". Jesus answered and said, "He that is washed needeth not save to wash his feet, but is clean every whit" [John 13:1-10].

Common sense would tell the reader that a man is not clean all over just, because his feet are washed. Therefore, he should either discard this story as fantastic or else look for its hidden meaning.

Every story of the Bible is a psychological drama taking place in the consciousness of man, and this one is no exception. This washing of the disciples' feet is the mystical story of spiritual circumcision or the revealing of the secrets of the Lord.

Jesus is called the Lord. You are told that the Lord's name is I AM – Je Suis. "I AM the Lord that is my name" [Isaiah 42:8]. The story states that Jesus was naked save for a towel which covered his loins or secrets. Jesus or Lord symbolizes your awareness of being whose secrets are hidden by the towel (consciousness of man). The foot symbolizes the understanding which must be washed of all human beliefs or conceptions of itself by the Lord. As the towel is removed to dry the feet, the secrets of the Lord are revealed.

In short, the removing of the belief that you are man reveals your awareness as the head of creation. Man is the foreskin hiding the head of creation. I AM the Lord hidden by the veil of man.

CHAPTER 15

Interval of Time

> *Let not your heart be troubled; ye believe in God, believe also in me. In my Father's house are many mansions; if it were not so, I would have told you. I go to prepare a place for you. And if I go and prepare a place for you, I will come again, and receive you unto myself; that where I am, there ye may be also.*
> —John 14:1-3

The ME in whom you must believe is your consciousness, the I AM; it is God. It is also the Father's house containing within itself all conceivable states of consciousness. Every conditioned state of consciousness is called a mansion.

This conversation takes place within yourself. Your I AM, the unconditioned consciousness, is the Christ Jesus speaking to the conditioned self or the John Smith consciousness.

"I AM John", from a mystical point of view, is two beings, namely, Christ and John.

So I go to prepare a place for you, moving from your present state of consciousness into that state desired. It is a promise by your Christ or awareness of being to your present conception of yourself that you will leave your present consciousness and appropriate another.

Man is such a slave to time that, if after he has appropriated a state of consciousness which is not now seen by the world and it, the appropriated state, does not immediately embody itself, he loses faith in his unseen claim; forthwith he drops it and returns to his former static state of being.

Because of this limitation of man, I have found it very helpful to employ a specified interval of time in making this journey into a prepared mansion.

Wait but a little while.

—Job 36:2

We have all catalogued the different days of the week, months of the year and seasons. By this, I mean you and I have said time and again, "Why, today feels just like Sunday" or "Monday" or "Saturday". We have also said in the middle of Summer, "Why, this feels and looks like the Fall of the year".

This is positive proof that you and I have definite feelings associated with these different days, months, and seasons of the year. Because of this association, we can at any time consciously dwell in that day or season which we have selected.

Do not selfishly define this interval in days and hours because you are anxious to receive it, but simply remain in the conviction that it is done – time, being purely relative, should be eliminated entirely – and your desire will be fulfilled.

This ability to dwell at any point in time permits us to employ time in our travel into the desired mansion.

Now I (consciousness) go to a point in time and there prepare a place. If I go to such a point in time and prepare a place, I shall return to this point in time where I have left; and I shall pick up and take you with me into that place which I have prepared, that where I AM, there ye may also be.

Let me give you an example of this travel.

Suppose you had an intense desire. Like most men who are enslaved by time, you might feel that you could not possibly realize so large a desire in a limited interval. But admitting that all things are possible to God, believing God to be the ME within you or your consciousness of being, you can say,

"As John, I can do nothing; but since all things are possible to God and God I know to be my consciousness of being, I can realize my desire in a little while. How my desire will be realized I do not (as John) know, but by the very law of my being I do know that it shall be."

With this belief firmly established, decide what would be a relative, rational interval of time in which such a desire could be realized.

Again, let me remind you not to shorten the interval of time because you are anxious to receive your desire; make it a natural interval. No one can give you the time interval. Only you can say what the natural interval would be to you. The interval of time is relative; that is, no two individuals would give the same measurement of time for the realization of their desire.

Time is ever conditioned by man's conception of himself. Confidence in yourself as determined by conditioned consciousness always shortens the interval of time.

If you were accustomed to great accomplishments, you would give yourself a much shorter interval in which to accomplish your desire than the man schooled in defeat.

If today were Wednesday and you decided that it would be quite possible for your desire to embody a new realization of yourself by Sunday, then Sunday becomes the point in time that you would visit.

To make this visit, you shut out Wednesday and let in Sunday. This is accomplished by simply feeling that it is Sunday. Begin to hear the church bells; begin to feel the quietness of the day and all that Sunday means to you; actually feel that it is Sunday.

When this is accomplished, feel the joy of having received that which on Wednesday was but a desire. Feel the complete thrill of having received it, and then return to Wednesday, the point in time you left behind you.

In doing this, you created a vacuum in consciousness by moving from Wednesday to Sunday. Nature, abhorring vacuums, rushes in to fill it, thereby fashioning a mould in the likeness of that which you potentially create, namely, the joy of having realized your defined desire.

As you return to Wednesday, you will be filled with a joyful expectancy, because you have established the consciousness of that which must take place the following Sunday.

As you walk through the interval of Thursday, Friday, and Saturday, nothing disturbs you regardless of conditions, because you predetermined that which you would be on the Sabbath and that remains an unalterable conviction.

Having gone before and prepared the place, you have returned to John and are now taking him with you through the interval of three days into the prepared place that he might share your joy with you, for where I AM, "there ye may also be".

CHAPTER 16

The Triune God

And God said, Let Us make man in Our image, after Our likeness.
—Gen. 1:26

Having discovered God to be our awareness of being and this unconditioned changeless reality (the I AM) to be the only creator, let us see why the Bible records a trinity as the creator of the world.

In the 26th verse of the first chapter of Genesis, it is stated:

And God said, Let Us make man in Our image.

The churches refer to this plurality of Gods as God the Father, God the Son, and God the Holy Spirit.

What is meant by "God the Father, God the Son, and God the Holy Spirit", they have never attempted to explain, for they are in the dark concerning this mystery.

The Father, Son, and Holy Spirit are three aspects or conditions of the unconditioned awareness of being called God.

The consciousness of being precedes the consciousness of being something. That unconditioned awareness which preceded all states of awareness is God – I AM.

The three conditioned aspects or divisions of itself can best be told in this manner:

The *receptive attitude of mind* is that aspect which receives impressions and therefore may be likened to a womb or Mother.

That which makes the impression is the male or pressing aspect and is therefore known as Father.

The impression in time becomes an *expression*, which expression is ever the likeness and image of the impression; therefore this objectified aspect is said to be the Son bearing witness of his Father-Mother.

An understanding of this mystery of the trinity enables the one who understands it to completely transform his world and fashion it to his own liking.

Here is a practical application of this mystery.

Sit quietly and decide what it is you would like most to express or possess. After you have decided, close your eyes and take your attention completely away from all that would deny the realization of the thing desired; then assume a receptive attitude of mind and play the game of supposing by imagining how you would feel if you were now to realize your desire.

Begin to listen as though space were talking to you and telling you that you are now that which you desire to be.

This receptive attitude is the state of consciousness that you must assume before an impression can be made.

As this pliable and impressive state of mind is attained, then begin to impress upon yourself the fact that you are that which you desired to be by claiming and feeling that you are now expressing and possessing that which you had decided to be and to have.

Continue in this attitude until the impression is made.

As you contemplate being and possessing that which you have decided to be and to have, you will notice that with every inhalation of breath a joyful thrill courses through your entire being.

This thrill increases in intensity as you feel more and more the joy of being that which you are claiming yourself to be.

Then in one final deep inhalation, your whole being will explode with the joy of accomplishment, and you will know by your feeling that you are impregnated by God, the Father.

As soon as the impression is made, open your eyes and return to the world that but a few moments before you had shut out.

In this receptive attitude of yours, while you contemplated being that which you desired to be, you were actually performing the spiritual act of generation; so you are now on your return from this silent meditation a pregnant being bearing a child or impression, which child was immaculately conceived without the aid of man.

Doubt is the only force capable of disturbing the seed or impression; to avoid a miscarriage of so wonderful a child, walk in secrecy through the necessary interval of time that it will take the impression to become an expression.

Tell no man of your spiritual romance. Lock your secret within you in joy, confident and happy that some day you will bear the son of your lover by expressing and possessing the nature of your impression.

Then will you know the mystery of "God said, 'Let Us make man in Our image'".

You will know that the plurality of Gods referred to is the three aspects of your own consciousness and that you are the trinity, meeting in a spiritual conclave to fashion a world in the image and likeness of that which you are conscious of being.

CHAPTER 17

Prayer

When thou prayest, enter into thy closet, and when thou hast shut thy door, pray to thy Father which is in secret; and thy Father which seeth in secret shall reward thee openly.
—Matt. 6:6

What things soever ye desire, when ye pray, believe that ye receive them, and ye shall have them.
—Mark 11:24

Prayer is the most wonderful experience man can have.
Unlike the daily murmurings of the vast majority of mankind in all lands who by their vain repetitions hope to gain the ear of God, prayer is the ecstasy of a spiritual wedding taking place in the deep, silent stillness of consciousness.

In its true sense prayer is God's marriage ceremony. Just as a maid on her wedding day relinquishes the name of her family to assume the name of her husband, in like manner, one who prays must relinquish his present name or nature and assume the nature of that for which he prays.

The gospels have clearly instructed man as to the performance of this ceremony in the following manner:

When ye pray go within in secret and shut the door and your Father who sees in secret will reward you openly.
—Matthew 6:6

The going within is the entering of the bridal chamber. Just as no one but the bride and groom are permitted to enter so holy a room as the bridal suite on the night of the marriage ceremony, likewise no one but the one who prays and that for which he prays are permitted to enter the holy hour of prayer. As the bride and groom on entering the bridal suite securely shut the door against the outside world, so too must the one who enters the holy hour of prayer close the door of the senses and entirely shut out the world round about him.

This is accomplished by taking the attention completely away from all things other than that with which you are now in love (the thing desired).

The second phase of this spiritual ceremony is defined in these words:

When ye pray, believe that ye receive, and ye shall receive.

As you joyfully contemplate being and possessing that which you desire to be and to have, you have taken this second step and are therefore spiritually performing the acts of marriage and generation.

Your receptive attitude of mind while praying or contemplating can be likened to a bride or womb for it is that aspect of mind which receives the impressions.

That which you contemplate being is the groom, for it is the name or nature you assume and therefore is that which leaves its impregnation; so one dies to maidenhood or present nature as one assumes the name and nature of the impregnation.

Lost in contemplation and having assumed the name and nature of the thing contemplated, your whole being thrills with the joy of being it. This thrill, which runs through your entire being as you appropriate the consciousness of your desire, is the proof that you are both married and impregnated.

As you return from this silent meditation, the door is once more opened upon the world you had left behind. But this time you return as a pregnant bride.

You enter the world a changed being and, although no one but you knows of this wonderful romance, the world will, in a very short while, see the signs of your pregnancy, for you will begin to express that which you in your hour of silence felt yourself to be.

The mother of the world or bride of the Lord is purposely called Mary, or water, for water loses its identity as it assumes the nature of that with which it is mixed. Likewise, Mary, the receptive attitude of mind, must lose its identity as it assumes the nature of the thing desired.

Only as one is willing to give up his present limitations and identity can he become that which he desires to be.

Prayer is the formula by which such divorces and marriages are accomplished.

> *Two shall agree as touching anything and it shall be established on earth.*
> —Matthew 18:19

The two agreeing are you, the bride, and the thing desired, the groom.

As this agreement is accomplished, a son bearing witness of this union will be born. You begin to express and possess that which you are conscious of being.

Praying, then, is recognizing yourself to be that which you desire to be rather than begging God for that which you desire.

Millions of prayers are daily unanswered because man prays to a God who does not exist.

Consciousness being God, one must seek in consciousness for the thing desired by assuming the consciousness of the quality desired. Only as one does this will his prayers be answered.

To be conscious of being poor while praying for riches is to be rewarded with that which you are conscious of being, namely, poverty.

Prayers, to be successful, must be claimed and appropriated. Assume the positive consciousness of the thing desired.

With your desire defined, quietly go within and shut the door behind you. Lose yourself in your desire; feel yourself to be one with it; remain in this fixation until you have absorbed the life and name by claiming and feeling yourself to be and to have that which you desired.

When you emerge from the hour of prayer, you must do so conscious of being and possessing that which you heretofore desired.

CHAPTER 18

The Twelve Disciples

And when He had called unto Him His twelve disciples, He gave them power against unclean spirits, to cast them out, and to heal all manner of sickness and all manner of disease.
—Matt. 10:1

The twelve disciples represent the twelve qualities of mind which can be controlled and disciplined by man. If disciplined, they will at all times obey the command of the one who has disciplined them.

These twelve qualities in man are potentials of every mind. Undisciplined, their actions resemble more the actions of a mob than they do of a trained and disciplined army. All the storms and confusions that engulf man can be traced directly to these twelve ill-related characteristics of the human mind in its present slumbering state.

Until they are awakened and disciplined, they will permit every rumor and sensuous emotion to move them.

When these twelve are disciplined and brought under control, the one who accomplishes this control will say to them, "Hereafter I call you not slaves, but friends."

Henceforth I call you not servants for the servant knoweth not what his lord doeth but I have called you friends, for all things that I have heard of My Father I have made known unto you.
—John 15:15

He knows that from that moment on, each acquired disciplined attribute of mind will befriend and protect him.

The names of the twelve qualities reveal their natures. These names are not given to them until they are called to discipleship.

They are: Simon, who was later surnamed Peter, Andrew, James, John, Philip, Bartholomew, Thomas, Matthew, James the son of Alphaeus, Thaddaeus, Simon the Canaanite, and Judas [Matthew 10; Mark 1; Mark 3; Luke 6].

The first quality to be called and disciplined is Simon, or the attribute of hearing.

This faculty, when lifted to the level of a disciple, permits only such impressions to reach consciousness as those which his hearing has commanded him to let enter. No matter what the wisdom of man might suggest or the evidence of his senses convey, if such suggestions and ideas are not in keeping with that which he hears, he remains unmoved. This one has been instructed by his Lord and made to understand that every suggestion he permits to pass his gate will, on reaching his Lord and Master (his consciousness), leave its impression there, which impression must in time become an expression.

The instruction to Simon is that he should permit only dignified and honorable visitors or impressions to enter the house (consciousness) of his Lord. No mistake can be covered up or hidden from his Master, for every expression of life tells his Lord whom he consciously or unconsciously entertained.

When Simon, by his works, proves himself to be a true and faithful disciple, then he receives the surname of Peter, or the rock, the unmoved disciple, the one who cannot be bribed or coerced by any visitor. He is called by his Lord Simon Peter, the one who faithfully hears the commands of his Lord and besides which commands he hears not.

It is this Simon Peter who discovers the I AM to be Christ, and for his discovery is given the keys to heaven, and is made the foundation stone upon which the Temple of God rests.

Buildings must have firm foundations and only the disciplined hearing can, on learning that the I AM is Christ, remain firm and unmoved in the knowledge that I AM Christ and beside ME there is no savior.

The second quality to be called to discipleship is Andrew, or courage.

As the first quality, faith in oneself, is developed, it automatically calls into being its brother, courage.

Faith in oneself, which asks no man's help but quietly and alone appropriates the consciousness of the quality desired and – in spite of reason or the evidence of his senses to the contrary continues faithful-patiently waiting in the knowledge that his unseen claim if sustained must be realized – such faith develops a courage and strength of character that are beyond the wildest dreams of the undisciplined man whose faith is in things seen.

The faith of the undisciplined man cannot really be called faith. For if the armies, medicines or wisdom of man in which his faith is placed be taken from him, his faith and courage go with it. But from the disciplined one the whole world could be taken and yet he would remain faithful in the knowledge that the state of consciousness in which he abides must in due season embody itself. This courage is Peter's brother Andrew, the disciple, who knows what it is to dare, to do and to be silent.

The next two (third & fourth) who are called are also related. These are the brothers, James and John. James the just, the righteous judge, and his brother John, the beloved.

Justice to be wise must be administered with love, ever turning the other cheek and at all times returning good for evil, love for hate, non-violence for violence.

The disciple James, symbol of a disciplined judgment, must, when raised to the high office of a supreme judge, be blindfolded that he may not be influenced by the flesh nor judge after the appearances of being. Disciplined judgment is administered by one who is not influenced by appearances.

The one who has called these brothers to discipleship continues faithful to his command to hear only that which he has been commanded to hear, namely, the Good.

The man who has this quality of his mind disciplined is incapable of hearing and accepting as true anything – either of himself or another – which does not on the hearing fill his heart with love.

These two disciples or aspects of the mind are one and inseparable when awakened.

Such a disciplined one forgives all men for being that which they are. He knows as a wise judge that every man perfectly expresses that which he is, as man, conscious of being.

He knows that upon the changeless foundation of consciousness all manifestation rests, that changes of expression can be brought about only through changes of consciousness.

With neither condemnation nor criticism, these disciplined qualities of the mind permit everyone to be that which he is. However, although allowing this perfect freedom of choice to all, they are nevertheless ever watchful to see that they themselves prophesy and do – both for others and themselves – only such things which when expressed glorify, dignify and give joy to the expresser.

The fifth quality called to discipleship is Philip.

This one asked to be shown the Father. The awakened man knows that the Father is the state of consciousness in which man dwells, and that this state or Father can be seen only as it is expressed.

He knows himself to be the perfect likeness or image of that consciousness with which he is identified.

So he declares, "No man has at any time seen My Father; but I, the Son, who dwelleth in His bosom have revealed Him."

No one has seen God at any time; the only begotten God who is in the bosom of the Father, He has explained Him; therefore, when you see Me, the Son, you see My Father, for I come to bear witness of My Father.

—John 1:18

If ye had known Me, ye should have known My Father also: and from henceforth ye know Him, and have seen Him.

—John 14-7

Have I been so long time with you, and yet hast thou not known Me, Philip? He that hath seen Me hath seen the Father; and how sayest thou then, Shew us the Father? Believest thou not that I am in the Father, and the Father in Me? The words that I speak unto you I speak not of Myself; but the Father that dwelleth in Me, He doeth the works. Believe Me that I am in the Father, and the Father in Me; or else believe Me for the very works' sake.
—John 14:9-11

I and My Father, consciousness and its expression, God and man, are one.

This aspect of the mind, when disciplined, persists until ideas, ambitions and desires become embodied realities. This is the quality which states "Yet in my flesh shall I see God" [Job 19:26].

It knows how to make the word flesh [John 1:14], how to give form to the formless.

The sixth disciple is called Bartholomew.

This quality is the imaginative faculty, which quality of the mind when once awake distinguishes one from the masses.

An awakened imagination places the one so awakened head and shoulders above the average man, giving him the appearance of a beacon light in a world of darkness. No quality so separates man from man as does the disciplined imagination.

This is the separation of the wheat from the chaff. Those who have given most to Society are our artists, scientists, inventors, and others with vivid imaginations.

Should a survey be made to determine the reason why so many seemingly educated men and women fail in their after-college years, or should it be made to determine the reason for the different earning powers of the masses, there would be no doubt but that imagination played the important part.

Such a survey would show that it is imagination which makes one a leader while the lack of it makes one a follower.

Instead of developing the imagination of man, our educational system oftentimes stifles it by attempting to put into the mind of man the wisdom he seeks. It forces him to memorize a number of text books which, all too soon, are disproved by later text books.

Education is not accomplished by putting something into man; its purpose is to draw out of man the wisdom which is latent within him. May the reader call Bartholomew to discipleship, for only as this quality is raised to discipleship will you have the capacity to conceive ideas that will lift you beyond the limitations of man.

The seventh is called Thomas.

This disciplined quality doubts or denies every rumor and suggestion that are not in harmony with that which Simon Peter has been commanded to let enter.

The man who is conscious of being healthy (not because of inherited health, diets or climate, but because he is awakened and knows the state of consciousness in which he lives) will, in spite of the conditions of the world, continue to express health.

He could hear, through the press, radio and wise men of the world that a plague was sweeping the earth and yet he would remain unmoved and unimpressed. Thomas, the doubter – when disciplined – would deny that sickness or anything else which was not in sympathy with the consciousness to which he belonged had any power to affect him.

This quality of denial – when disciplined – protects man from receiving impressions that are not in harmony with his nature. He adopts an attitude of total indifference to all suggestions that are foreign to that which he desires to express. Disciplined denial is not a fight or a struggle but total indifference.

Matthew, the eighth, is the gift of God.

This quality of the mind reveals man's desires as gifts of God.

The man who has called this disciple into being knows that every desire of his heart is a gift from heaven and that it contains both the power and the plan of its self-expression.

Such a man never questions the manner of its expression. He knows that the plan of expression is never revealed to man for God's ways are past finding out [Romans 11:33].

He fully accepts his desires as gifts already received and goes his way in peace confident that they shall appear.

The ninth disciple is called James, the son of Alphaeus.

This is the quality of discernment. A clear and ordered mind is the voice which calls this disciple into being.

This faculty perceives that which is not revealed to the eye of man. This disciple judges not from appearances for it has the capacity to function in the realm of causes and so is never misled by appearances.

Clairvoyance is the faculty which is awakened when this quality is developed and disciplined; not the clairvoyance of the mediumistic séance rooms, but the true clairvoyance or clear seeing of the mystic. That is, this aspect of the mind has the capacity to interpret that which is seen. Discernment or the capacity to diagnose is the quality of James the son of Alphaeus.

Thaddaeus, the tenth, is the disciple of praise, a quality in which the undisciplined man is woefully lacking.

When this quality of praise and thanksgiving is awake within man, he walks with the words "Thank you, Father" ever on his lips.

He knows that his thanks for things not seen opens the windows of heaven and permits gifts beyond his capacity to receive to be poured upon him.

The man who is not thankful for things received is not likely to be the recipient of many gifts from the same source.

Until this quality of the mind is disciplined, man will not see the desert blossom as the rose. Praise and thanksgiving are to the invisible gifts of God (one's desires) what rain and sun are to the unseen seeds in the bosom of the earth.

The eleventh quality called is Simon of Canaan.

A good key phrase for this disciple is "hearing good news". Simon of Canaan, or Simon from the land of milk and honey, when called to discipleship, is proof that the one who calls this faculty into being has become conscious of the abundant life. He can say with the Psalmist David, "Thou preparest a table before me in the presence of mine enemies; thou anointest my head with oil; my cup runneth over" [Psalm 23:5]. This disciplined aspect of the mind is incapable of hearing anything other than good news and so is well qualified to preach the Gospel or Good-spell.

The twelfth and last of the disciplined qualities of the mind is called Judas.

When this quality is awake, man knows that he must die to that which he is before he can become that which he desires to be.

So it is said of this disciple that he committed suicide, which is the mystic's way of telling the initiated that Judas is the disciplined aspect of detachment.

This one knows that his I AM or consciousness is his savior, so he lets all other saviors go.

This quality – when disciplined – gives one the strength to let go.

The man who has called Judas into being has learned how to take his attention away from problems or limitations and to place it upon that which is the solution or savior.

Except ye be born again, you cannot in anywise enter the Kingdom of Heaven.

Truly, truly, I say to you, unless one is born again, he cannot see the kingdom of God.

—John 3:3

No greater love hath man than this, that he give his life for a friend.

Greater love hath no man than this, that a man lay down his life for his friends.

—John 15:13

When man realizes that the quality desired, if realized, would save and befriend him, he willingly gives up his life (present conception of himself) for his friend by detaching his consciousness from that which he is conscious of being and assuming the consciousness of that which he desires to be.

Judas, the one whom the world in its ignorance has blackened, will, when man awakes from his undisciplined state, be placed on high; for God is love and no greater love has a man than this – that he lay down his life for a friend.

Until man lets go of that which he is now conscious of being, he will not become that which he desires to be; and Judas is the one who accomplishes this through suicide or detachment.

These are the twelve qualities which were given to man in the foundation of the world.

Man's duty is to raise them to the level of discipleship. When this is accomplished, man will say:

I have finished the work which thou gavest Me to do. I have glorified Thee on earth and now, o, Father, glorify Thou Me with Thine own Self with the glory which I had with Thee before the world was.

—John 17:4, 5

CHAPTER 19

Liquid Light

In Him we live and move, and have our being.
—Acts 17:28

Psychically, this world appears as an ocean of light containing within itself all things, including man, as pulsating bodies enveloped in liquid light.

The Biblical story of the Flood [Genesis 6-8] is the state in which man lives.

Man is actually inundated in an ocean of liquid light in which countless numbers of light-beings move.

The story of the Flood is really being enacted today.

Man is the Ark containing within himself the male-female principles of every living thing.

The dove or idea which is sent out to find dry land is man's attempt to embody his ideas. Man's ideas resemble birds in flight – like the dove in the story, returning to man without finding a place to rest.

If man will not let such fruitless searches discourage him, one day the bird will return with a green sprig. After assuming the consciousness of the thing desired, he will be convinced that it is so; and he will feel and know that he is that which he has consciously appropriated, even though it is not yet confirmed by his senses.

One day man will become so identified with his conception that he will know it to be himself, and he will declare, "I AM; I AM that which

I desire to be (I AM that I AM)". He will find that, as he does so, he will begin to embody his desire (the dove or desire will this time find dry land), thereby realizing the mystery of the word made flesh.

Everything in the world is a crystallization of this liquid light. "I AM the light of the world" [John 8:12, John 9:5, John 12:46].

Your awareness of being is the liquid light of the world, which crystallizes into the conceptions you have of yourself.

Your unconditioned awareness of being first conceived itself in liquid light (which is the initial velocity of the universe). All things, from the highest to the lowest vibrations or expressions of life, are nothing more than the different vibrations of velocities of this initial velocity; gold, silver, iron, wood, flesh etc., are only different expressions or velocities of this one substance-liquid light.

All things are crystallized liquid light; the differentiation or infinity of expression is caused by the conceiver's desire to know himself.

Your conception of yourself automatically determines the velocity necessary to express that which you have conceived yourself to be.

The world is an ocean of liquid light in countless different states of crystallization.

CHAPTER 20

The Breath of Life

Then the LORD God formed man of dust from the ground, and breathed into his nostrils the breath of life; and man became a living being.
—Genesis 2:7

As thou knowest not what is the way of the spirit, nor how the bones do grow in the womb of her that is with child, even so thou knowest not the works of God who maketh all.

Just as you don't know how the breath of life enters the limbs of a child within its mother's womb, you also don't understand how God, who made everything, works.
—Ecclesiastes 11:5

And it came to pass after these things that the son of the woman, the mistress of the house, fell sick; and his sickness was so sore, that there was no breath left in him.
—1 Kings 17:17

And he (Elisha) went up and lay upon the child, and put his mouth upon his mouth, and his eyes upon his eyes, and his hands upon his hands, and stretched himself upon the child; and the flesh of the child waxed warm.
—2 Kings 4:34

But after the three and a half days, the breath of life from God came into them, and they stood on their feet; and great fear fell upon those who were watching them.
 —Revelation 11:11

Did the Prophet Elijah [and/or Elisha] really restore to life the dead child of the Widow?

This story, along with all the other stories of the Bible, is a psychological drama which takes place in the consciousness of man.

The Widow symbolizes every man and woman in the world; the dead child represents the frustrated desires and ambitions of man; while the prophet, Elijah [and/or Elisha], symbolizes the God power within man, or man's awareness of being.

The story tells us that the prophet took the dead child from the Widow's bosom and carried him into an upper room. As he entered this upper room he closed the door behind them. Placing the child upon a bed, he breathed life into him. Returning to the mother, he gave her the child and said,

Woman, thy son liveth.

See, thy son liveth.
 —1 Kings 17:23, 2 Kings 4:36

Man's desires can be symbolized as the dead child. The mere fact that he desires is positive proof that the thing desired is not yet a living reality in his world. He tries in every conceivable way to nurse this desire into reality, to make it live, but finds in the end that all attempts are fruitless.

Most men are not aware of the existence of the infinite power within themselves as the prophet. They remain indefinitely with a dead child in their arms, not realizing that the desire is the positive indication of limitless capacities for its fulfillment.

Let man once recognize that his consciousness is a prophet who breathes life into all that he is conscious of being, and he will close the door of his senses against his problem and fix his attention – solely on that which he desires, knowing that by so doing, his desires are certain to be realized.

He will discover recognition to be the breath of life, for he will perceive – as he consciously claims himself to be now expressing or possessing all he desires to be or to have – that he will be breathing the breath [sic!] of life into his desire.

The quality claimed for the desire (in a way unknown to him) will begin to move and become a living reality in his world.

Yes, the Prophet Elijah [and/or Elisha] lives forever as man's limitless consciousness of being, the widow as his limited consciousness of being and the child as that which he desires to be.

CHAPTER 21

Daniel in the Lions' Den

Thy God whom thou servest continually; He will deliver thee.
—Daniel 6:16

The story of Daniel is the story of every man. It is recorded that Daniel, while locked in the lions' den, turned his back upon the hungry beasts; and with his vision turned toward the light coming from above, he prayed to the one and only God. The lions, who were purposely starved for the feast, remained powerless to hurt the prophet. Daniel's faith in God was so great that it finally brought about his freedom and his appointment to a high office in the government of his country [Daniel 6:13-28].

This story was written for you to instruct you in the art of freeing yourself from any problem or prison in the world.

Most of us on finding ourselves in the lions' den would be concerned only with the lions; we would not be thinking of any other problem in the whole wide world but that of lions. Yet, we are told that Daniel turned his back upon them and looked toward the light that was God. If we could follow the example of Daniel while threatened with any dire disaster such as lions, poverty or sickness, if, like Daniel, we could remove our attention to the light that is God, our solutions would be similarly simple.

For example, if you were imprisoned, no man would need to tell you that what you should desire is freedom. Freedom or rather the desire to be free would be automatic. The same would be true if you found yourself sick or in debt or in any other predicament.

Lions represent seemingly unsoluble situations of a threatening nature.

Every problem automatically produces its solution in the form of a desire to be free from the problem.

Therefore, turn your back upon your problem and focus your attention upon the desired solution by already feeling yourself to be that which you desire.

Continue in this belief, and you will find that your prison wall will disappear as you begin to express that which you have become conscious of being.

I have seen people, apparently hopelessly in debt, apply this principle, and in but a very short time, debts that were mountainous were removed. I have also seen those whom doctors had given up as uncurable apply this principle, and in an incredibly short time, their so-called incurable disease vanished and left no scar.

Look upon your desires as the spoken words of God and every word of prophecy of that which you are capable of being. Do not question whether you are worthy or unworthy to realize these desires. Accept them as they come to you. Give thanks for them as though they were gifts. Feel happy and grateful for having received such wonderful gifts. Then go your way in peace.

Such simple acceptance of your desires is like the dropping of fertile seed into an ever-prepared soil.

When you drop your desire in consciousness as a seed, confident that it shall appear in its full-blown potential, you have done all that is expected of you. To be worried or concerned about the manner of their unfoldment is to hold these fertile seeds in a mental grasp and, therefore, to prevent them from really maturing to full harvest.

Don't be anxious or concerned as to results. Results will follow just as surely as day follows night.

Have faith in this planting until the evidence is manifest to you that it is so. Your confidence in this procedure will pay great rewards. You wait but a little while in the consciousness of the thing desired;

then suddenly, and when you least expect it, the thing felt becomes your expression. Life is no respecter of persons [Acts 10:34; Romans 2:11] and destroys nothing; it continues to keep alive that which man is conscious of being.

Things will disappear only as man changes his consciousness. Deny it if you will, it still remains a fact that consciousness is the only reality and things but mirror that which you are conscious of being.

The heavenly state you seek will be found only in consciousness for the Kingdom of Heaven is within you.

Your consciousness is the only living reality, the eternal head of creation. That which you are conscious of being is the temporal body that you wear.

To turn your attention from that which you are aware of being is to decapitate that body; but, just as a chicken or snake continues to jump and throb for a while after its head has been removed, likewise qualities and conditions appear to live for a while after your attention has been taken from them.

Man, not knowing this law of consciousness, constantly gives thought to his previous habitual conditions and, through being attentive to them, places upon these dead bodies the eternal head of creation; thereby he reanimates and re-resurrects them.

You must leave these dead bodies alone and let the dead bury the dead [Matthew 8:22, Luke 9:60].

Man, having put his hand to the plough (that is, after assuming the consciousness of the quality desired), by looking back, can only defeat his fitness for the Kingdom of Heaven [Luke 9:62].

As the will of heaven is ever done on earth, you are today in the heaven that you have established within yourself, for here on this very earth your heaven reveals itself.

The Kingdom of Heaven really is at hand. Now is the accepted time. So create a new heaven, enter into a new state of consciousness and a new earth will appear.

CHAPTER 22

Fishing

They went forth, and entered into a ship, and that night they caught nothing.

—John 21:3

And He said unto them, Cast the net on the right side of the ship, and ye shall find. They cast therefore, and now they were not able to draw it for the multitude of fishes.

—John 21:6

It is recorded that the disciples fished all night and caught nothing. Then Jesus appeared upon the scene and told them to cast their nets again, but, this time, to cast them on the right side. Peter obeyed the voice of Jesus and cast his nets once more into the waters. Where but a moment before the water was completely empty of fish, the nets almost broke with the number of the resulting catch [John 21:3-6].

Man, fishing all through the night of human ignorance, attempts to realize his desires through effort and struggle only to find in the end that his search is fruitless. When man discovers his awareness of being to be Christ Jesus, he will obey its voice and let it direct his fishing. He will cast his hook on the right side; he will apply the law in the right manner and will seek in consciousness for the thing desired. Finding it there, he will know that it will be multiplied in the world of form.

Those who have had the pleasure of fishing know what a thrill it is to feel the fish upon the hook. The bite of the fish is followed by the play of the fish; this play, in turn, is followed by the landing of the fish.

Something similar takes place in the consciousness of man as he fishes for the manifestations of life.

Fishermen know that if they wish to catch big fish, they must fish in deep waters; if you would catch a large measure of life, you must leave behind you the shallow waters with its many reefs and barriers and launch out into the deep blue waters where the big ones play.

To catch the large manifestations of life you must enter into deeper and freer states of consciousness; only in these depths do the big expressions of life live.

Here is a simple formula for successful fishing.

First, decide what it is you want to express or possess. This is essential.

You must definitely know what you want of life before you can fish for it. After your decision is made, turn from the world of sense, remove your attention from the problem and place it on just being, by repeating quietly but with feeling, "I AM".

As your attention is removed from the world round about you and placed upon the I AM, so that you are lost in the feeling of simply being, you will find yourself slipping the anchor that tied you to the shallows of your problem; and effortlessly you will find yourself moving out into the deep.

The sensation which accompanies this act is one of expansion. You will feel yourself rise and expand as though you were actually growing. Do not be afraid of this floating, growing experience for you are not going to die to anything but your limitations.

However, your limitations are going to die as you move away from them for they live only in your consciousness.

In this deep or expanded consciousness, you will feel yourself to be a mighty pulsating power as deep and as rhythmical as the ocean. This expanded feeling is the signal that you are now in the deep blue waters where the big fish swim. Suppose the fish you decided to catch were health and freedom; you begin to fish in this formless pulsating depth of yourself for these qualities or states of consciousness by feeling "I AM healthy", "I AM free".

You continue claiming and feeling yourself to be healthy and free until the conviction that you are so possesses you. As the conviction is born within you, so that all doubts pass away and you know and feel that you are free from the limitations of the past, you will know that you have hooked these fish.

The joy which courses through your entire being on feeling that you are that which you desired to be is equal to the thrill of the fisherman as he hooks his fish.

Now comes the play of the fish. This is accomplished by returning to the world of the senses.

As you open your eyes on the world round about you, the conviction and the consciousness that you are healthy and free should be so established within you that your whole being thrills in anticipation.

Then, as you walk through the necessary interval of time that it will take the things felt to embody themselves, you will feel a secret thrill in knowing that in a little while that which no man sees, but that which you feel and know that you are, will be landed.

In a moment when you think not, while you faithfully walk in this consciousness, you will begin to express and possess that which you are conscious of being and possessing; experiencing with the fisherman the joy of landing the big one.

Now, go and fish for the manifestations of life by casting your nets in the right side.

CHAPTER 23

Be Ears That Hear

Let these sayings sink down into your ears; For the Son of Man shall be delivered into the hands of men.
—Luke 9:44

Be not as those who have eyes that see not and ears that hear not. Let these revelations sink deep into your ears, for after the Son (idea) is conceived, man with his false values (reason) will attempt to explain the why and wherefore of the Son's expression, and in so doing, will rend him to pieces.

After men have agreed that a certain thing is humanly impossible and therefore cannot be done, let someone accomplish the impossible thing; the wise ones who said it could not be done will begin to tell you why and how it happened. After they are all through tearing the seamless robe [John 19:23] (cause of manifestation) apart, they will be as far from the truth as they were when they proclaimed it impossible. As long as man looks for the cause of expression in places other than the expresser, he looks in vain.

For thousands of years, man has been told:

I AM the resurrection and the life.
—John 11:25

No manifestation cometh unto me save I draw it.
—John 6:44

But man will not believe it. He prefers to believe in causes outside of himself.

The moment that which was not seen becomes seen, man is ready to explain the cause and purpose of its appearance.

Thus, the Son of Man (idea desiring manifestation) is constantly being destroyed at the hands of man (reasonable explanation or wisdom).

Now that your awareness is revealed to you as cause of all expression, do not return to the darkness of Egypt with its many gods. There is but one God. The one and only God is your awareness.

And all the inhabitants of the earth are reputed as nothing. And He doeth according to His will in the army of Heaven and among the inhabitants of the earth, and none can stay His hand, or say unto him 'what doest Thou?'

All the inhabitants of the earth are accounted as nothing; but He does according to His will in the host of heaven and among the inhabitants of earth. And no one can ward off His hand or say to Him, 'What have You done?'

—Daniel 4:35

If the whole world should agree that a certain thing could not be expressed and yet you became aware of being that which they had agreed could not be expressed, you would express it.

Your awareness never asks permission to express that which you are aware of being. It does so, naturally and without effort, in spite of the wisdom of man and all opposition.

Salute no man by the way.

Carry no money belt, no bag, no shoes; and greet no one on the way.

—Luke 10:4; 2Kings 4:29

This is not a command to be insolent or unfriendly, but a reminder not to recognize a superior, not to see in anyone a barrier to your expression.

None can stay your hand or question your ability to express that which you are conscious of being.

Do not judge after the appearances of a thing, "for all are as nothing in the eyes of God."

> *All the nations are as nothing before Him. They are regarded by Him as less than nothing and meaningless.*
> —Isaiah 40:17

When the disciples, through their judgment of appearances, saw the insane child [Mark 9:17-29; Luke 9:37-43], they thought it a more difficult problem to solve than others they had seen; and so they failed to achieve a cure.

In judging after appearances, they forgot that all things were possible to God [Matthew 19:26; Mark 10:27]. Hypnotized as they were by the reality of appearances, they could not feel the naturalness of sanity.

The only way for you to avoid such failures is to constantly bear in mind that your awareness is the Almighty, the all-wise presence. Without help, this unknown presence within you effortlessly outpictures that which you are aware of being.

Be perfectly indifferent to the evidence of the senses, so that you may feel the naturalness of your desire, and your desire will be realized. Turn from appearances and feel the naturalness of that perfect perception within yourself, a quality never to be distrusted or doubted. Its understanding will never lead you astray.

Your desire is the solution of your problem. As the desire is realized, the problem is dissolved.

You cannot force anything outwardly by the mightiest effort of the will. There is only one way you can command the things you want and that is by assuming the consciousness of the things desired.

There is a vast difference between feeling a thing and merely knowing it intellectually. You must accept without reservation the fact that by possessing (feeling) a thing in consciousness, you have commanded the reality that causes it to come into existence in concrete form.

You must be absolutely convinced of an unbroken connection between the invisible reality and its visible manifestation. Your inner acceptance must become an intense, unalterable conviction which transcends both reason and intellect, renouncing entirely any belief in the reality of the externalization except as a reflection of an inner state of consciousness. When you really understand and believe these things, you will have built up so profound a certainty that nothing can shake you.

Your desires are the invisible realities which respond only to the commands of God. God commands the invisible to appear by claiming himself to be the thing commanded.

He made Himself equal with God and found it not robbery to do the works of God.
—Philippians 2:6

Now let this saying sink deep in your ear:

BE CONSCIOUS OF BEING THAT WHICH YOU WANT TO APPEAR.

CHAPTER 24

Clairvoyance

Having eyes, see ye not? And having ears, hear ye not? And do ye not remember?
—Mark 8:18

True clairvoyance rests, not in your ability to see things beyond the range of human vision, but rather in your ability to understand that which you see.

A financial statement can be seen by anyone, but very few can read a financial statement. The capacity to interpret the statement is the mark of clear seeing or clairvoyance.

That every object, both animate and inanimate, is enveloped in a liquid light which moves and pulsates with an energy far more radiant than the objects themselves, no one knows better than the author; but he also knows that the ability to see such auras is not equal to the ability to understand that which one sees in the world around about him.

To illustrate this point, here is a story with which the whole world is familiar, yet only the true mystic or clairvoyant has ever really seen it.

SYNOPSIS

The story of Dumas' "Count of Monte Cristo" is, to the mystic and true clairvoyant, the biography of every man.

I

Edmond Dantés, a young sailor, finds the captain of his ship dead. Taking command of the ship in the midst of a storm-swept sea, he attempts to steer the ship into a safe anchorage.

COMMENTARY

Life itself is a storm-swept sea with which man wrestles as he tries to steer himself into a haven of rest.

II

On Dantés is a secret document which must be given to a man he does not know, but who will make himself known to the young sailor in due time. This document is a plan to set the Emperor Napoleon free from his prison on the Isle of Elba.

COMMENTARY

Within every man is the secret plan that will set free the mighty emperor within himself.

III

As Dantés reaches port, three men (who by their flattery and praise have succeeded in worming their way into the good graces of the present king), fearing any change that would alter their positions in the government, have the young mariner arrested and committed to the catacombs.

COMMENTARY

Man in his attempt to find security in this world is misled by the false lights of greed, vanity and power.

Most men believe that fame, great wealth or political power would secure them against the storms of life. So they seek to acquire these as the anchors of their life, only to find that in their search for these they gradually lose the knowledge of their true being. If man places his faith in things other than himself, that in which his faith is placed, will in time destroy him; at which time he will be as one imprisoned in confusion and despair.

IV

Here in this tomb, Dantés is forgotten and left to rot. Many years pass. Then one day, Dantés (who is by this time a living skeleton) hears a knock on his wall. Answering this knock, he hears the voice of one on the other side of the stone. In response to this voice, Dantés removes the stone and discovers an old priest who has been in prison so long that no one knows the reason for his imprisonment or the length of time he has been there.

COMMENTARY

Here behind these walls of mental darkness, man remains in what appears to be a living death. After years of disappointment, man turns from these false friends, and he discovers within himself the ancient one (his awareness of being) who has been buried since the day he first believed himself to be man and forgot that he was God.

V

The old priest had spent many years digging his way out of this living tomb only to discover that he had dug his way into Dantés' tomb. He then resigns himself to his fate and decides to find his joy and freedom by instructing Dantés in all that he knows concerning the mysteries of life and to aid him to escape as well.

Dantés, at first, is impatient to acquire all this information; but the old priest, with infinite patience garnered through his long imprisonment, shows Dantés how unfit he is to receive this knowledge in his present, unprepared, anxious mind. So, with philosophic calm, he slowly reveals to the young man the mysteries of life and time.

COMMENTARY

This revelation is so wonderful that when man first hears it he wants to acquire it all at once; but he finds that, after numberless years spent in the belief of being man, he has so completely forgotten his true identity that he is now incapable of absorbing this memory all at once. He also discovers that he can do so only in proportion to his letting go of all human values and opinions.

VI

As Dantés ripens under the old priest's instructions, the old man finds himself living more and more in the consciousness of Dantés. Finally, he imparts his last bit of wisdom to Dantés, making him competent to handle positions of trust. He then tells him of an inexhaustible treasure buried on the Isle of Monte Cristo.

COMMENTARY

As man drops these cherished human values, he absorbs more and more of the light (the old priest), until finally he becomes the light and knows himself to be the ancient one. I AM the light of the world.

VII

At this revelation, the walls of the catacomb which separated them from the ocean above cave in, crushing the old man to death. The guards, discovering the accident, sew the old priest's body into a sack and prepare to cast it out to sea. As they leave to get a stretcher, Dantés removes the body of the old priest and sews himself into the bag. The guards, unaware of this change of bodies, and believing him to be the old man, throw Dantés into the water.

COMMENTARY

The flowing of both blood and water in the death of the old priest is comparable to the flow of blood and water from the side of Jesus as the Roman soldiers pierced him, the phenomenon which always takes place at birth (here symbolizing the birth of a higher consciousness).

VIII

Dantés frees himself from the sack, goes to the Isle of Monte Cristo and discovers the buried treasure. Then, armed with this fabulous wealth and this superhuman wisdom, he discards his human identity of Edmond Dantés and assumes the title of the Count of Monte Cristo.

COMMENTARY

Man discovers his awareness of being to be the inexhaustible treasure of the universe. In that day, when man makes this discovery, he dies as man and awakes as God.

Yes, Edmond Dantés becomes the Count of Monte Cristo. Man becomes Christ.

CHAPTER 25

Twenty Third Psalm

I

The Lord is my Shepherd; I shall not want.

COMMENTARY

My awareness is my Lord and Shepherd. That which I AM aware of being is the sheep that follow me. So good a shepherd is my awareness of being, it has never lost one sheep or thing that I AM aware of being.

My consciousness is a voice calling in the wilderness of human confusion; calling all that I AM conscious of being to follow me.

So well do my sheep know my voice, they have never failed to respond to my call; nor will there come a time when that which I am convinced that I AM will fail to find me.

I AM an open door for all that I AM to enter.

My awareness of being is Lord and Shepherd of my life. Now I know I shall never be in need of proof or lack the evidence of that which I am aware of being. Knowing this, I shall become aware of being great, loving, wealthy, healthy and all other attributes that I admire.

II

He maketh me to lie down in green pastures.

COMMENTARY

My awareness of being magnifies all that I am aware of being, so there is ever an abundance of that which I am conscious of being.

It makes no difference what it is that man is conscious of being, he will find it eternally springing in his world.

The Lord's measure (man's conception of himself) is always pressed down, shaken together and running over.

III

He leadeth me beside the still waters.

COMMENTARY

There is no need to fight for that which I am conscious of being, for all that I am conscious of being shall be led to me as effortlessly as a shepherd leads his flock to the still waters of a quiet spring.

IV

He restoreth my soul; He leadeth me in the paths of righteousness for His Name's sake.

COMMENTARY

Now that my memory is restored – so that I know I AM the Lord and beside me there is no God – my kingdom is restored.

My kingdom – which became dismembered in the day that I believed in powers apart from myself – is now fully restored.

Now that I know my awareness of being is God, I shall make the right use of this knowledge by becoming aware of being that which I desire to be.

V

Yea, though I walk through the valley of the shadow of death, I will fear no evil; for Thou art with me; Thy rod and Thy staff, they comfort me.

COMMENTARY

Yes, though I walk through all the confusion and changing opinions of men, I will fear no evil, for I have found consciousness to be that which makes the confusion. Having in my own case restored it to its rightful place and dignity, I shall, in spite of the confusion, outpicture that which I am now conscious of being. And the very confusion will echo and reflect my own dignity.

VI

Thou preparest a table before me in the presence of mine enemies; Thou anointest my head with oil; my cup runneth over.

COMMENTARY

In the face of seeming opposition and conflict, I shall succeed, for I will continue to outpicture the abundance that I am now conscious of being.

My head (consciousness) will continue to overflow with the joy of being God.

VII

Surely goodness and mercy shall follow me all the days of my life; and I will dwell in the house of the Lord forever.

COMMENTARY

Because I am now conscious of being good and merciful, signs of goodness and mercy are compelled to follow me all the days of my life, for I will continue to dwell in the house (or consciousness) of being God (good) forever.

CHAPTER 26

Gethsemane

Then cometh Jesus with them unto a place called Gethsemane, and saith unto the disciples, Sit ye here, while I go and pray yonder.

—Matt. 26:36

A most wonderful mystical romance is told in the story of Jesus in the Garden of Gethsemane, but man has failed to see the light of its symbology and has mistakenly interpreted this mystical union as an agonizing experience in which Jesus pleaded in vain with His Father to change His destiny.

Gethsemane is, to the mystic, the Garden of Creation – the place in consciousness where man goes to realize his defined objectives. Gethsemane is a compound word meaning to press out an oily substance; Geth, to press out, and Shemen, an oily substance.

The story of Gethsemane reveals to the mystic, in dramatic symbology, the act of creation.

Just as man contains within himself an oily substance which, in the act of creation, is pressed out into a likeness of himself, so he has within himself a divine principle (his consciousness) which conditions itself as a state of consciousness and without assistance presses out or objectifies itself.

A garden is a cultivated piece of ground, a specially prepared field, where seeds of the gardener's own choice are planted and cultivated.

Gethsemane is such a garden, the place in consciousness where the mystic goes with his properly defined objectives. This garden is entered when man takes his attention from the world round about him and places it on his objectives.

Man's clarified desires are seeds containing the power and plans of self-expression and, like the seeds within man, these, too, are buried within an oily substance (a joyful, thankful attitude of mind).

As man contemplates being and possessing that which he desires to be and to possess, he has begun the process of pressing out or the spiritual act of creation.

These seeds are pressed out and planted when man loses himself in a wild, mad state of joy, consciously feeling and claiming himself to be that which he formerly desired to be.

Desires expressed, or pressed out, result in the passing of that particular desire. Man cannot possess a thing and still desire to possess it at one and the same time. So, as one consciously appropriates the feeling of being the thing desired, this desire to be the thing passes – is realized.

The receptive attitude of mind, feeling, and receiving the impression of being the thing desired, is the fertile ground or womb which receives the seed (defined objective).

The seed which is pressed out of a man grows into the likeness of the man from whom it was pressed.

Likewise, the mystical seed, your conscious claim that you are that which you heretofore desired to be, will grow into the likeness of you from whom and into whom it is pressed.

Yes, Gethsemane is the cultivated garden of romance where the disciplined man goes to press seeds of joy (defined desires) out of himself into his receptive attitude of mind, there to care for and nurture them by consciously walking in the joy of being all that formerly he desired to be.

Feel with the Great Gardener the secret thrill of knowing that things and qualities not now seen will be seen as soon as these conscious impressions grow and ripen to maturity.

Your consciousness is Lord and Husband [Isaiah 54:5]; the conscious state in which you dwell is wife or beloved. This state made visible is your son bearing witness of you, his father and mother, for your visible world is made in the image and likeness [Genesis 2:26] of the state of consciousness in which you live; your world and the fullness thereof are nothing more or less than your defined consciousness objectified.

Knowing this to be true, see to it that you choose well the mother of your children – that conscious state in which you live, your conception of yourself.

The wise man chooses his wife with great discretion. He realizes that his children must inherit the qualities of their parents and so he devotes much time and care to the selection of their mother. The mystic knows that the conscious state in which he lives is the choice that he has made of a wife, the mother of his children, that this state must in time embody itself within his world; so he is ever select in his choice and always claims himself to be his highest ideal.

He consciously defines himself as that which he desires to be.

When man realizes that the conscious state in which he lives is the choice that he has made of a mate, he will be more careful of his moods and feelings. He will not permit himself to react to suggestions of fear, lack or any undesirable impression. Such suggestions of lack could never pass the watch of the disciplined mind of the mystic, for he knows that every conscious claim must in time be expressed as a condition of his world – of his environment.

So, he remains faithful to his beloved, his defined objective, by defining and claiming and feeling himself to be that which he desires to express. Let a man ask himself if his defined objective would be a thing of joy and beauty if it were realized.

If his answer is in the affirmative, then he may know that his choice of a bride is a princess of Israel, a daughter of Judah, for every defined objective which expresses joy when realized is a daughter of Judah, the king of praise.

Jesus took with Him into His hour of prayer His disciples, or disciplined attributes of mind, and commanded them to watch while He prayed, so that no thought or belief that would deny the realization of His desire might enter His consciousness.

Follow the example of Jesus, who, with His desires clearly defined, entered the Garden of Gethsemane (the state of joy) accompanied by His disciples (His disciplined mind) to lose Himself in a wild joy of realization.

The fixing of His attention on His objective was His command to His disciplined mind to watch and remain faithful to that fixation. Contemplating the joy that would be His on realizing His desire, He began the spiritual act of generation, the act of pressing out the mystical seed – His defined desire. In this fixation He remained, claiming and feeling Himself to be that which He (before He entered Gethsemane) desired to be, until His whole being (consciousness) was bathed in an oily sweat (joy) resembling blood (life); in short, until His whole consciousness was permeated with the living, sustained joy of being His defined objective.

As this fixation is accomplished so that the mystic knows by his feeling of joy that he has passed from his former conscious state into his present consciousness, the Passover or Crucifixion is attained.

This crucifixion or fixation of the new conscious claim is followed by the Sabbath, a time of rest. There is always an interval of time between the impression and its expression, between the conscious claim and its embodiment. This interval is called the Sabbath, the period of rest or non-effort (the day of entombment).

To walk unmoved in the consciousness of being or possessing a certain state is to keep the Sabbath.

The story of the crucifixion beautifully expresses this mystical stillness or rest. We are told that after Jesus cried out, "It is finished!" [John 19:30], He was placed in a tomb. There He remained for the entire Sabbath.

When the new state or consciousness is appropriated so, you feel by this appropriation fixed and secure in the knowledge that it is finished; then you, too, will cry out, "It is finished!" and will enter the tomb or Sabbath, an interval of time in which you will walk unmoved in the conviction that your new consciousness must be resurrected (made visible).

Easter, the day of resurrection, falls on the first Sunday after the full moon in Aries. The mystical reason for this is simple. A defined area will not precipitate itself in the form of rain until this area reaches the point of saturation; just so the state in which you dwell will not express itself until the whole is permeated with the consciousness that it is so – it is finished.

Your defined objective is the imaginary state, just as the equator is the imaginary line across which the sun must pass to mark the beginning of spring. This state, like the moon, has no light or life of itself; but will reflect the light of consciousness or sun.

I am the light of the world.
—Matthew 5:14; John 8:12; John 9:5; John 12:46

I am the resurrection and the life.
—John 11:25

As Easter is determined by the full moon in Aries, so too is the resurrection of your conscious claim determined by the full consciousness of your claim, by actually living as this new conception.

Most men fail to resurrect their objectives because they fail to remain faithful to their newly defined state until this fullness is attained.

If man would bear in mind the fact that there can be no Easter or day of resurrection until after the full moon, he would realize that the state into which he has consciously passed will be expressed or resurrected only after he has remained within the state of being his defined objective.

Until his whole self thrills with the feeling of actually being his conscious claim — in consciously living in this state of being it and only in this way – will man ever resurrect or realize his desire.

CHAPTER 27

A Formula for Victory

Every place that the sole of your foot shall tread upon, that have I given unto you.

—Joshua 1:3

The majority of people are familiar with the story of Joshua capturing the city of Jericho. What they do not know is that this story is the perfect formula for Victory, under any circumstances and against all odds.

It is recorded that Joshua was armed only with the knowledge that every place that the sole of his foot should tread upon would be given to him; that he desired to capture or tread upon the city of Jericho but found the walls separating him from the city impassable.

It seemed physically impossible for Joshua to get beyond these massive walls and stand upon the city of Jericho. Yet, he was driven by the knowledge of the promise that, regardless of the barriers and obstacles separating him from his desires, if he could but stand upon the city, it would be given to him.

The Book of Joshua further records that instead of fighting this giant problem of the wall, Joshua employed the services of the harlot, Rahab, and sent her as a spy into the city. As Rahab entered her house, which stood in the midst of the city, Joshua – who was securely barred by the impassable walls of Jericho – blew on his trumpet seven times. At the seventh blast, the walls crumbled and Joshua entered the city victoriously.

To the uninitiated, this story is senseless. To the one who sees it as a psychological drama, rather than as a historical record, it is most revealing.

If we would follow the example of Joshua, our victory would be similarly simple.

Joshua symbolizes to you, the reader, your present state; the city of Jericho symbolizes your desire, or defined objective.

The walls of Jericho symbolize the obstacles between you and the realization of your objectives. The foot symbolizes the understanding; placing the sole of the foot upon a definite place indicates fixing a definite psychological state.

Rahab, the spy, is your ability to travel secretly or psychologically to any place in space. Consciousness knows no frontier. No one can stop you from dwelling psychologically at any point, or in any state in time or space.

Regardless of the physical barriers separating you from your objective, you can, without effort or help of anyone, annihilate time, space and barriers.

Thus, you can dwell, psychologically, in the desired state. So, although you may not be able to tread physically upon a state or city, you can always tread psychologically upon any desired state. By treading psychologically, I mean that you can now, this moment, close your eyes, and after visualizing or imagining a place or state other than your present one, actually FEEL that you are now in such a place or state. You can feel this condition to be so real that upon opening your eyes you are amazed to find that you are not physically there.

A harlot, as you know, gives to all men that which they ask of her. Rahab, the harlot, symbolizes your infinite capacity to psychologically assume any desirable state without questioning whether or not you are physically or morally fit to do so.

You can today capture the modern city of Jericho or your defined objective if you will psychologically re-enact this story of Joshua; but to capture the city and realize your desires, you must carefully follow the formula of victory as laid down in this book of Joshua.

This is the application of this victorious formula as a modern mystic reveals it today:

First: Define your objective—not the manner of obtaining it, but your objective, pure and simple; know exactly what it is you desire so that you have a clear mental picture of it.

Secondly: Take your attention away from the obstacles which separate you from your objective and place your thought on the objective itself.

Thirdly: Close your eyes and FEEL that you are already in the city or state that you would capture. Remain within this psychological state until you get a conscious reaction of complete satisfaction in this victory. Then, by simply opening your eyes, return to your former conscious state.

This secret journey into the desired state, with its subsequent psychological reaction of complete satisfaction, is all that is necessary to bring about total victory.

This victorious psychical state will embody itself despite all opposition. It has the plan and power of self-expression.

From this point forward, follow the example of Joshua, who, after psychologically dwelling in the desired state until he received a complete conscious reaction of victory, did nothing more to bring about this victory than to blow seven times on his trumpet.

The seventh blast symbolizes the seventh day, a time of stillness or rest, the interval between the subjective and objective states, a period of pregnancy or joyful expectancy.

This stillness is not the stillness of the body but rather the stillness of the mind – a perfect passivity, which is not indolence but a living stillness born of trust in this immutable law of consciousness.

Those not familiar with this law or formula for victory, in attempting to still their minds, succeed only in acquiring a quiet tension, which is nothing more than compressed anxiety.

But you, who know this law, will find that after capturing the psychological state which would be yours if you were already victoriously and actually entrenched in that city, will move forward towards the physical realization of your desires.

You will do this without doubt or fear, in a state of mind fixed in the knowledge of a pre-arranged victory.

You will not be afraid of the enemy, because the outcome has been determined by the psychological state that preceded the physical offensive; and all the forces of heaven and earth cannot stop the victorious fulfillment of that state.

Stand still in the psychological state defined as your objective until you feel the thrill of Victory.

Then, with confidence born of the knowledge of this law, watch the physical realization of your objective.

Set your self, stand still, and watch the salvation of the Lord with you...

—2 Chronicles 20:17

THE CREATIVE USE
OF IMAGINATION

PREFACE

This book, as all things, came into being because of a thought acted upon. Neville left us October 1, 1972 and, since that time, I have invested many hours transcribing the hundreds of tapes I have of his lectures. Neville explained that the ark of life contained and could be understood on three levels: the literal, psychological and spiritual. The lectures which are available deal mainly with the spiritual. However, because those who are now hearing his words on tapes and reading his lectures, did not hear him speak on the second (or psychological) level, I realized the need to provide that psychological plane as a foundation for the higher, spiritual level. And so, the thought was planted in my mind. What if there were some lectures that taught this principle on a practical level? Wouldn't it be wonderful if such a series could be found and made available for those who would desire it. And then one day I received a letter from a lovely lady in San Francisco who said she was moving into a retirement home and wanted to send me some notes she had from Neville's lecture series in San Francisco in 1952. These notes constitute this book.

I had a thought. Wouldn't it be wonderful if... and acted upon it by feeling the thrill of the thought's completion. I have never met the lady or heard from her since receiving the notes, but I have proved, once again, that imagination (thought) fulfills itself. The living proof is in your hands.

Now, let me tell you a bit about me. Born and raised in a small town in Kansas, I moved to California in 1942 as a good Protestant. But I had a hunger that no organized religion could fill, so I drifted from one belief to another, seeking yet not finding what I was searching for, possibly because I did not know what it was. Then one day I heard a man called Neville, and I knew that, although the outer me did not understand his words, the inner me was singing the Hallelujah Chorus, for I had found the cause of all life.., that my very thought, mixed with feeling, was an imaginal act which created the facts in my world.

I remember the first night I lay in my bed and dared to claim, "I AM God." Afraid that the ceiling would crash down on me, I quickly covered my head—just in case. And when nothing happened, I gathered more courage and set out to prove for myself that imagination could create reality. I did not believe it could, and I wanted to prove Neville wrong. That was back in 1964, and I haven't succeeded yet. Not all of my imaginal acts have come to fruition, but I now know that the fault does not lie in the teaching, but in my belief in myself. And, as I have grown in my belief and trust and faith in what I have imagined, I have gained confidence in my own wonderful human imagination.

Several years ago, I put together a group of lectures of Neville's and called the book "Immortal Man." At the time, I was afraid to change his words even though felt I could make the message clearer if I did.

Shortly after its publication, I turned to self one night and asked, "Is it all right to change the words as long as I do not change the meaning? I know that if truth were told so that it could be understood, it would be believed. I know your words are true, Neville, but think I can make them clearer." I fell asleep questioning myself and, in the night, I had this dream: I am on my way to work. As I enter the building I see, directly before me, a beautiful restaurant whose tables are filled with diners, enjoying their meal. Neville is standing next to a fireplace, speaking to a group nearby. Thrilled to find him there, I am eager to show him the book of his lectures I had just published and question him regarding the change of words. But as I turn to take the case I am carrying into my office, get the book and return, he glances up and catches my eye. Instantly changing my mind, I turn and go directly into the restaurant to join him. But when I arrive, I discover that he has vanished, leaving the ladies to tell me that he is gone and will never return again.

Heartsick, I return to the lobby with its hard, tile floor when, suddenly the case I had been carrying fell from its handle. The moment it hit the floor, the case opened, my book fell out and lay open at its center seam. As I looked down in horror, I saw that I had been carrying a brief ease which contained a tape recorder that had turned on due to the fall, and Neville's voice was ringing out loud and clear. Embarrassed, I stooped down to turn off the volume, only to discover that all the knobs had fallen off the machine and there was no way for me to turn him off. As I tried to push the case over to the far wall in order to pick it up, I awoke with these words ringing in my ears, "I am IN you, AS you." From that moment on, my fears have vanished and, since that time, I have gained confidence in my writing. These are Neville's words - Neville's thoughts - yet we are so closely woven in the tapestry of thought that the words are now mine.

The lectures you will read are Neville's words, yet they may not have been the exact words he spoke back in 1952. The material I had to work with were notes someone had taken in shorthand, transcribed, and duplicated. I have taken the notes and elaborated on them. The words are true and, hopefully understandable enough so you can test them and discover for yourself that when the truth is applied, it is made alive by a spiritual experience.

Always bear in mind that when Neville speaks of "man," he is speaking of generic man (man/woman). Man is the external world, the natural man; while imagination is the internal world, the man of spirit. God (imagination) became the natural man that the man of nature may become God who is Spirit.

Always think of yourself as two beings, one who sees through the organs of sense and the other who sees through the mind of imagination. And always remember God's name as he revealed it to Moses. "I AM. That is who I AM. And by this name, I shall be known throughout all generations. I AM that I AM." I the trinity, in unthinkable origin, AM God the Father. And I in creative expression AM the Son, for imagination is born of consciousness. Therefore I, in universal interpretation, in infinite imminence, in eternal procession AM God, the Holy Spirit.

Margaret Ruth Broome

CHAPTER 1
Your Infinite Worth

The purpose of these talks is to bring about a psychological change in you, the individual. Humanity, understood psychologically, is an infinite series of levels of awareness and you, individually, are what you are according to where you are in the series. Consciousness is the only reality, and where you are conscious of being psychologically, determines the circumstances of your life. The ancients knew this great truth, but our modern teachers have yet to discover it. There is only one substance in the world. Our scientists call it energy while scripture defines it as consciousness. We are told that the universe was caused by water, but if this is true, then it could not evolve into anything but water. But if the basic substance is energy (or consciousness), it can be made to manifest itself as iron, steel and wood, to name but a few. Man, seeing a variety of forms, thinks of numberless substances, but what is seen is only a change in the arrangement of the same basic substance—consciousness.

Ephesians tells us that, "All things, when admitted, are made manifest by light." The word "light" recorded here means awareness; consciousness." The state the individual admits into his consciousness is the cause of one man being rich and another poor. The poor man admits to being in the state of poverty by saying, "I am poor," just as the rich man admits wealth by saying, "I am rich." Anything you, an individual, claim yourself to be (be it good, bad or indifferent, right or wrong) must be made manifest in your world, for by claiming the state, you have consented to its life.

There is only one cause, and that is consciousness. Your consciousness is the center from which your world mirrors and echoes the state you presently occupy. Now, a state can be defined as all that you believe and consent to as being true. So, if you want your world to change, you must determine what you want to accept and consent to as true before you can change it. To arrive at a certain definition of self, you must begin by uncritically observing your automatic reaction to an event, for your reaction defines your state. And you can, without getting out of your chair, rebuild your world by changing your level (or state) of being. This is done by observing yourself uncritically as you react to life. If you do not like the circumstances of your life, acknowledge its cause. Be willing to admit that the circumstances are only objectifying what you are conscious of, then change your consciousness and your world will change. If you react to that which is being objectified, you bind yourself to a certain, level of awareness, but if you refuse to react, the thread is broken. Stop being conscious of something unlovely, for every unlovely thought causes you to walk in psychological mud. Rather, identify yourself with beauty, with love (the Christ in you) and you will ascend the infinite level of your own being and change the circumstances of your life.

Your state of awareness, like a magnet, attracts life. Steel, in its demagnetized state is a whirling mass of electrons, but when the electrons are faced in one direction, the steel is magnetized. You do not add to the steel to make it magnetic or take anything away to demagnetize it. This same principle is true for you. You can change your world by rearranging your thoughts and having them travel only in one direction, and that is toward the fulfillment of your desire.

Watch your reactions to life, for any change in the arrangement of your mind which can be detected by self-observation, will cause a change in your outer world. It is important to learn to be passive to that which is unlovely and unacceptable to you. In that way, you are awakening the dynamic one within. And when you find your inner being, you will discover that the qualities you condemn in others are really in yourself. Then you will know the secret of forgiveness, for as you forgive yourself, the others are forgiven.

All things (not just a few) are made manifest by the light, and everything manifested is light. The moment you consent to a thought, it is made manifest. It could not come into being unless you consented to its expression by being aware of it. The universe moves with motiveless necessity as it has no motive of its own. Rather, it moves under the necessity of manifesting the arrangements of the minds of men. This teaching is to awaken you to your light, and the awakening begins by self-observation.

If you have a secret affection for living in the mud of self-pity and condemnation, your world will mirror those feelings. But if you will rearrange your mind and live in the heavenly feeling of harmony and love, your manifested world will change. If, today, you would spend five minutes in uncritical observation of yourself, you would be surprised to discover how deceitful you are. It is a terrible shock, I know, but every shock of this type will let in the light of awareness, and life is an ever-increasing illumination. As the light comes in, you become more and more conscious of who you really are.

There is only one cause for the phenomena of life. Only by observing your own consciousness can you discover the cause of what is happening to you. There is no greater tyrant than the belief in a secondary cause. Let that tyrant go by remembering the one and only substance; the only cause which is awareness and immediately change what you are aware of. Only by observing your reactions to life can you find yourself. And remember, as long as you react as you do, the same things must confront you, for all that you admit to is made manifest by your consciousness, and everything you manifest is your consciousness.

Stop walking through the world in the mud and living in its basement. Your soul is made up of all that you consent to. Lose your soul on one level and you will find it on a higher level, defined differently. Always examine yourself uncritically, for the moment you become critical, you automatically justify your reactions and associate yourself with the thing observed. Everything is individual. Collective security and collective salvation are terms approached individually. Learn to stand on your own feet and not on the feet of a group. You must free yourself, and the only way to do that is to awaken the Christ in you who is sound asleep. Think noble thoughts based on noble concepts and they will pay great dividends, for you will rise in consciousness and transform your world. Give yourself your daily bread by giving yourself the opportunity to remember who you are! Never envy the good fortune of another, simply appropriate your own. "Be transformed by the renewing of your mind" by changing the ideas planted there, for you cannot change your thinking until you change the ideas from which your thoughts flow.

CHAPTER 2

Take Not the Name in Vain

Your individual state of consciousness is your level of being and attracts all of the events you encounter in life. Since your reactions determine what you are, any change in your outer world must be produced by your inner level of being.

In the 7th Chapter of the Book of Mark, we are told, "Hear and understand: there is nothing outside which can defile man; but what comes out of a man's mind is what defiles him. He who has ears, let him hear." Now, thoughts are things. When you identify yourself with a thought, it outpictures itself as an act. If the thought is unlovely, it defiles you. Awaken and select only thoughts that contribute to the birth of your desire. You must constantly observe your dwelling place, for where you are psychologically is what you are. Your mood indicates your state, and you are always externalizing the state upon which you stand.

The Upanishads, one of a class of Vedic treatises dealing with broad philosophic problems, states: "The soul, imagining itself into a state, takes upon itself the results of that state. Not imagining itself into the state, it is free from its results." Your soul is what you consent to. As you feel yourself into the situation of your answered prayer, you have entered a state and your soul has taken upon itself the results of that state. If you do not enter the state, you are free of its lovely results. Accept an idea as true. Identify yourself with it and it will outpicture itself in your world. But if you do not accept the thought and identify yourself with it through feeling, you are free from its results. You must become very selective and learn not to associate yourself with unlovely thoughts.

In the Book of Kings, we are told how those who entered the temple brought something alive with them such as an ox or bullock. These were used as burnt offerings. These sacrifice offerings are your body of suffering. They are the animals you must offer called grievances. No matter what the grievance may be, you have no right to carry it around with you and you cannot ascend in consciousness until all of your grievances are tossed on the altar and sacrificed. Only as you give them up will you find the holy water.

Now, this holy water is not the church variety but the symbol of the twelve aspects of the mind. When your mind is cleared of all of its cobwebs (grievances), the bowl of holy water is placed on the backs of oxen, and your disciplined mind serves you rather than you serving it. The bull symbolizes the mind in its wild state and must be tamed (washed in holy water and clothed in soft raiment). When you enter the Holy of holies alone and bathe in its waters, your mind is washed of all mean thoughts and cleansed. Begin now to associate your thoughts only with the good; then that which proceeds out of your mouth (mind) will never defile you.

I AM is the self-definition of the infinite. "Go and tell them that I AM has sent me unto you. Awareness (I AMness) is the only power of the universe. Its power makes you alive. If you say, "I am sick," you are! If you say, "I am secure," you are! Feeling yourself into the situation of a given state, you must take upon yourself the results of that state of mind. All things are made alive from a state of mind and without the state nothing can be made, as you only resurrect the state from which you are identified. Where you are psychologically is what you are in reality. Therefore, if you catch yourself feeling sorry for yourself, stop it and start feeling happy. If you don't, you will identify yourself with the state of self-pity and outpicture it.

"Let the weak man say, 'I am strong.'" Don't wait until you become strong before saying this. If you feel weak in any sense, affirm "I am strong," and if you persist in that assumption it will harden into fact. No one should ever take the name of the Lord in vain, for that name is I AM.

The righteous man is already conscious of being the person he wants to be. He never sins, but runs into the name, for sinning is missing his desired state, and righteousness is hitting it. "I will set him on high because he knows my name." Assume the consciousness of being the one you want to be and you will be saved from your present state. Your individual hunger can and will be satisfied when you run righteously into the state desired. This is done through the act of feeling. Feel happy and you are conscious of happiness. Feel married and you have consciously moved into the state of marriage. The thing desired must be felt before you are conscious of possessing it.

Learn to say "no" to unlovely thoughts rather than accepting them with passive indifference, for a soul must imagine himself into the act to taste the fruit of the state acted upon. Remember, consciousness alone is the cause of the fruit you reap and the only explanation for its existence.

There is no one to blame but self for all of the things that have happened, are happening and will happen to you, as they could not come into your world unless you consented to them. Start now to consent only to lovely thoughts of fulfilled desires prior to their confirmation by your senses, and give up the animal instinct of suffering and bathing yourself in the feelings of hurt and self-pity.

The psychological tongue is much like the physical one. If someone annoys you, turn aside and keep the tongue of your mind away from the sore spots of dislike, for your little mental conversations are the producers of your future. Sacrifice your body of suffering by giving it up and tame your mind, for we are told, "Blessed are the meek (tame), for they shall inherit the earth." Clothe yourself with joy and good news and you will walk into your holy of holies clothed in your immortal garment of love.

There is a rhythm in your world which you cannot hear or see, and your aura is like no one else's. A bloodhound knows. If two odors were alike, no bloodhound could find you. But you are unique, one of a kind with your own special aura radiating your level of being. Don't judge auras for the simple reason that you have to see the aura of another through your own, and what you are seeing is only your assumption of the man.

Complacency is a curse. "Blessed are they that hunger and thirst after righteousness." Control your imagination with steady attention and dare to stand and be heard. Andrew is the disciple who symbolizes this aspect of mind. Pay attention to your thoughts and discipline them so that they flow from the feeling of your wish fulfilled, for you are not awake until the outer you becomes placid and the inner you dynamic.

Don't try to argue someone out of their misery. We are told to, "Let the filthy be filthy still; what is that to thee? Follow thou me." Man is given the power of the "I" to think, and everyone is allowed to think for himself.

All things, when admitted to consciousness, are made manifest, be they good, bad or indifferent. Dare to stand on your own by this teaching and you will never again feel the need to justify failure.

CHAPTER 3

Desire

As you are, so shall God appear to be to you. The priest will see God as the head of all celestial and terrestrial records. To a judge, he is the great judge forever meting out punishment. To the Hottentot, God is the kind of chief he, himself, would like to be. So, you see, men are forever creating God in their own image.

"God is God from the creation. Truth alone is man's salvation. But the God that now you worship soon shall be your God no more.

For the soul in its unfolding Evermore its thoughts remolding and it learns more truly in its progress whom to love and how to adore." Through this teaching, you will learn to outgrow your concept of God, for God changes not, only your ideas of Him change.

Desire is your mainspring of action, for you cannot move without desire. Ask yourself, "What wantest thou of me?" and then formulate your desire. Feel its presence and you have granted yourself the desire's fulfillment. Human life is nothing more than the appeasement of hunger, and the infinite series of levels of awareness is the means to satisfy that hunger. Health is a desire, a hunger which can be appeased when the idea is formulated in the mind that I am healthy. The same is true for wealth, peace, harmony or fame, for all of these are states of awareness. Identify yourself with the state desired. Persist in this identification and, because you and God are one consciousness, what you are conscious of, you outpicture.

The cross is the symbol of suffering. There is no physical cross upon which a man was nailed, but a body of beliefs which a man wears.

"Except you deny yourself and lift up your cross and follow me, you are unworthy of me." Lift up your cross by raising your awareness, for your I AMness is the creator of your world.

As an individual, you move and live in time, but your true being is in eternity. Think of the vertical line of the cross as the line of being upon which there are unnumbered levels of awareness. Now, time cannot make you better or wiser. In fact, time cannot do a thing towards changing your level of being, for change is all on the vertical line where you move to higher or lower levels of your own being. Because change is imminent, we speak of it as infinite imminence; as nearer than near and sooner than now. The man you would like to be is imminent. He is nearer than near. The ideal you dream of being is sooner than now and is brought into being by a change in your reactions to life.

In the Book of Revelations, we are told, "I will give to every being according to his work." The only work you are called upon to do is work on yourself. Start this work by observing your reactions to life. Remember, your future is not being developed, it already is. The time track is complete as well as all of the events you can encounter. As you move up or down the level of your being, changes will occur in your life. You are now resting at a certain level. "Arise, take up your couch and walk," by breaking the threads of life that bind you to the state you are now in. Break these threads by changing your thoughts, for only as you rise within, will you find a corresponding change without.

Have you ever wondered what it would be like if you were of too pure eyes to behold iniquity? If you were all tenderness? All love? All generosity? Aim for those feelings and then watch your relationship to them. It is here, in the midst of the storms of life, that you work this law. If you identify yourself with an unlovely state, you will find yourself sinking into it. But you can lift up your cross by breaking your automatic, mechanical reactions to life and sacrificing your present level of being.

This message comes, not to bring peace, but a sword. It comes to set a man at variance against his brother, father, mother and all the members of his household, for I bring the sword of truth which is the word of God. This word is sharper than any two-edged sword, for it is capable of piercing the soul and spirit. I am not suggesting that you turn against your earthly relatives, but that you turn against the psychological ideas that govern your behavior and the dominant mood which governs your actions and reactions to life. If, at this moment your feelings are not noble, turn against them, for they are your psychological mother. This is done by putting new feeling in their place. You cannot change your thinking until you change your feeling, and all feelings come from ideas. A man's enemies are those of his own household which is everything he accepts as true.

This sword can pierce, even to the severing of soul and spirit. Your Father (your I AM) is Spirit, and when you worship Him, you must do so in spirit and in truth. Be still and say to yourself, with feeling "I AM He."

All that you consent to, all that you believe and accept as true (be it wise or foolish) forms the clothing you wear. But you can be reclothed and ascend to a higher level of being when you take up your cross and follow your imagination.

Most of us are aimless. We want more than we presently have. We want the other fellow to change, but we don't want to do the one thing that will bring the change about, for we don't want to change self. In Revelations, John tells us, "I will give to everyone according to his work." The gift is not given according to the work of another, but according to the work you do on yourself, and that work is to uncritically observe your reactions to life, as they bind you to a certain level. Disassociate yourself from your unpleasant thoughts and associate yourself with your aim, thereby rising to its level, for your ideal is on that vertical line you stand upon.

Scripture tells us to "Seek and you shall find: and when you find him, you will be like him." I tell you, you will never find your fulfilled desire until you are the desire! Those who go searching for love only make manifest their lovelessness, for you never have to search for what you are!

I am Mary and you are Mary too, for we are forever conceiving of ourselves. The whole of human life is the appeasement of desire, and desire, conceived as fulfilled, will externalize itself. If you are not hungry enough to transcend your present level of consciousness, you will not conceive of anything greater. As long as you are in love with the state you are in, you cannot and will not rise from it.

Without the vertical line of states, life would have no meaning. The ancients called this infinite series, Jacob's ladder. You do not build this ladder, rather you climb it through self-discovery.

When you think of another, you are seeing only your opinion of him. If you think he is kind, he is kind. If you think he is stupid, he is stupid as he is playing the part you have assigned him because of your opinion. Therefore, if your desire is for him to change, you must change your opinion of yourself, for "he" is only your opinion pushed out.

Where you are psychologically is what you are; therefore, only associate with the feeling that leads you to the fulfillment of your dreams. And may all of your dreams be noble ones.

CHAPTER 4

Are You Making Wine?

The Bible's purpose is to lift the individual up to a higher level of being. This begins in the state of Moses and the discovery of I AM. Then, in the Book of Isaiah, we are told to "Turn back your foot from the sabbath and take delight in the Lord." Let us examine this thought to find its deeper meaning. Now, in order to keep the sabbath, you must cease from having any mental doubt, as the mental foot you stand upon is your belief. When your mental foot touches the earth, its action is automatic and mechanical. Using your powerful consciousness, begin now to break the mechanical hold it has on your life by turning your thoughts to your fulfilled desire and observe the sabbath.

The twins spoken of in scripture symbolize your duality: Abel, the inner you, and Cain, the outer you. A reversal of order must now occur, for in the New Testament your true identity is revealed as Christ (the inner you) your hope of glory.

As you walk the earth, see people as they want to be seen, and you are pouring oil on their wounds. But if you do not, you are as the scribes and the Pharisees described in the 23rd Chapter of Matthew, doing their deeds to be seen by men; they preach but do not practice.

In the 3rd Chapter of the Book of John, the story is told of Nicodemus, an intellectual man who believed that if he kept the law of Moses he could enter the kingdom of heaven, yet he was told, "You must be born again, born of water and spirit." Here we see the difference between the intellect and wisdom. Keeping the law of Moses is not enough. You must experience a change in the level of your being, thereby giving you wisdom in order for you to know rebirth.

Your inner talking is the breeding ground of your future, be it lovely or unlovely. This is told us so vividly in the Book of Deuteronomy: "I set before you this day blessings and cursings." Every time you tell someone off, even though it is done in your mind, you curse him. And every time you do unto others what you would like done unto you, they are blessed in the doing.

Water is the symbol of psychological truth. To know the truth is not enough. It must be acted upon, at which time the psychological water turns into wine.

Start now to observe all of your unpleasant, negative thoughts and change them, for until you separate yourself from the state from which these thoughts flow, they will continue to cause you to have the same experiences in life.

CHAPTER 5

Seeing God

St. Augustine once said, "O, my God, let me see thee, and if to die is to see thee, then let me die that I may behold thy face." Yet, when we fell God told us, "You cannot see my face and live. But I will cause my glory to pass by and when I pass by, you shall see my back, but my face you will not see." That God is your wonderful I AMness, your awareness who is forever claiming, "I AM that is who I AM." Imagination's power is the only power. It is your power to kill, to make alive, to wound and to heal. It is your imagination which forms the light, makes the good, and creates the evil, and there is no other God. Man is inclined to believe in two powers, one for good and the other for evil, but I tell you there is only one. The "I" in man is he who kills and makes alive, who curses and creates. Your consciousness of being is the only reality. The self-definition of an absolute state is "I am divine." And this absolute state is God. It is your I AM which cannot be seen.

Matthew tells us, "Blessed are the pure in heart for they shall see God." The word "pure" in the above statement comes from the Greek word "katharos" which also means, "clean; clear." To be pure, the mind must be cleared of all obstructions created by traditional wrong thinking. The heart must be cleared of the belief in a secondary power. Only when this is done will you be blessed, for you will know the one and only God to be your true self.

There is no power outside of you. The same power in you that makes the good, creates the evil. Start now to free yourself from the belief in two powers, for only then will you be pure in heart and see God.

The whole vast universe is nothing more than the response to the consciousness of men. If you believe that the "I" in another is the cause of your displeasure and not your own "I," then you have planted a tree in your mind which is obstructing your view and must be uprooted. We are told, "No man shall imagine evil in his heart." I am not speaking of a physical organ, but of the mind, the center or heart of the matter. When your heart is pure, you become a member of the order of Melchizedek. Read the story carefully and you will see that when Abraham slaughtered the kings (all of his negative and unlovely ideas), he returned to find Melchizedek, the symbol of the I AM, the being you really are.

Learn to discipline your mind, for only the disciplined mind can maintain the feeling of the wish fulfilled. If, what you had imagined has not come into being, it is because you have not severed the ties that bind you to the level where you now stand. You must break your mechanical reaction to life in order to change your life-track.

The only reason for this teaching is to encourage you and push you up the vertical line of the cross. It is very important for you to learn to be uncritical of yourself, for if you are not, you will justify your behavior which will cause you to remain in your present state. But if you will stop being critical, you will stop the negative thoughts that bind you to your present state and move out of it into another.

There are three ways to clear your mind of the trees of traditional wrong thinking and allow you to see God. They are: uncritical observation; non-identification; and sacrifice of the state you formerly believed yourself to be. Man tries to see God by means of little pictures, but God can only be seen through belief in one power. Through uncritical observation, you will encounter your particular state. If you don't like the role the state requires you to play as it unfolds, stop reacting to it. Until you reach the point where you no longer react, you are not pure enough to see God. When you see Him, you will know Him, as you will be like Him.

Where "I" AM is always what "I" AM. Establish one "I" within yourself, not a number of "I's." The "I" roots out all secondary causes and clears the mind of the power to enslave. Your belief in powers external to you is a tree which must be rooted out of your mind.

Begin now to use this technique and you will realize your every dream. But first you must have a dream, a desire for something, as desire is your springboard of action. Define your objective. If it were fulfilled now, where would you be physically? What would the world look like? Would your wife, husband, mother, father, or friends see you differently? Feel their presence: see the joy expressed on their faces, and hear their congratulations. Repeat this act until you have the feeling of accomplishment. Then, having assumed the feeling of completion, remain faithful to it, for your assumption contains within itself all of the plans and power necessary for externalization. You need do nothing on the outside, for by your assumption, your mind is being rearranged, and what it confirms, it externalizes. Your desire may be for an improvement in your financial position, your social circle, or a deeper understanding of the mystery. The desire is up to you, but when put into practice, this technique will never fail you.

The kingdom of heaven, with its many states (some lovely and some not so lovely) is within you. The state capable of wounding or healing, killing or making alive, is within you. They are all psychological states, completely furnished and ready to externalize themselves in your world. And, if having entered a particular mansion (state), you do not care to remain there, you may leave it by the same technique it was entered - through the act of assumption.

It is so easy to feel sorry for yourself and so very difficult to give up this feeling. But you cannot enter another state until you do. No one can uproot the weeds of self-pity or the trees of so-called second causes for you. You must uproot them yourself. God put Adam in the garden to tend and keep it. As Adam you fell asleep, but when you awake, you are Christ, the power and the wisdom of God. Start now to observe your reactions to life and do not allow yourself to become identified with any unlovely state. Sacrifice your little hurts, your grievances, and belief in secondary causes. Then you will be blessed, for you will be pure in heart and see God.

Awake! Test yourself and you will discover that the fault you see in the other exists in you. Turn to self, and you will find the Christ in you who is your hope of glory.

CHAPTER 6

All Is Consciousness

Blessed are you when your mental comprehension has been enlarged by the removal of the trees of traditional wrong thinking, for only then will you know that all is consciousness and consciousness is all. You will know that any secondary cause is a tyrant, and if you believe in an outside power, you are fighting a losing battle.

Emerson once said, "Man surrounds himself with the true image of himself, as every spirit builds for itself a house beyond its house, a world beyond its world." What you are, that only can you see. Therefore, build yourself a world as you would like it to be—a world beyond the world now visible to you. The world you desire exists and will unfold itself in great proportions when you, all spirit, surround yourself with the true image of yourself as you would like to be. Think of your world as a canvas with the pictures painted there by the arrangement of your mind. Your I AMness (consciousness) has already arranged as many patterns for your canvas as there are people walking the earth. Turn to yourself and, claiming that your desire exists, feel yourself move right into its center. Then paint your canvas of consciousness. Everything is there at your disposal. Its reality is up to you and the intensity of your desire. Always look to self, for your consciousness is the sole cause of the phenomena of your individual life.

Perhaps you have imagined something which never came to pass and you feel that you failed, but I tell you there is only one cause for failure and that is absence of the feeling of naturalness. It takes time for an assumption to become a fact, and a desire is fulfilled proportionate to the degree of naturalness of the feeling of possession. If something does not feel natural to you, it is not your nature. To ask in my name is to ask in my nature or character; therefore, when you ask, you must feel you already are that which you are seeking.

"Whatsoever you desire, when you pray, believe that you have received it, and you will." It is important to feel yourself right into your wish fulfilled, for consciousness is the only reality, and everything you see is nothing more than an outpicturing of a state of consciousness. It is stupid to seek a thing before you establish its cause. An effect depends upon a state of consciousness, and you cannot find the effect without being its cause. And if you do not feel the naturalness of the desired state, you cannot externalize it, for consciousness is very observable.

Ask yourself how long you have been conscious of being what you want to be. To what extent do you feel its reality now? Matthew tells us, "0, you faithless and perverse generation. How long shall I be with you?" Do you have faith in what you are conscious of? I hope so, for without faith it is impossible to achieve anything. It is the substance of the thing hoped for and the cause of all phenomena. The word "perverse" means "to turn the wrong way; without aim, fixity or one-pointedness of purpose." When the latest headline or news bulletin can turn you from your desire, you are perverse and fail. But if success is your goal, its mood must be worn until the feeling of being successful is so natural you cannot turn away from it.

On the other hand, "importunity" means "brazen impudence." If you will so persist in your assumption, your brazen impudence will not allow you to accept the evidence of your senses when they deny your assumption, but will rearrange the substance called life into the pattern of your assumption. This world moves with the necessity of molding and manifesting the arrangement of the individual's mind. It is important to persist until fulfillment becomes your nature. Changes begin to occur at their moment of naturalness. Jacob told the Lord, "I will not let you go until you bless me." As Jacob, you may wrestle through the night with an idea (and all ideas come down from heaven to take flesh). If you will not take no for an answer but persist in the feeling of your wish fulfilled, you will be blessed with its externalization.

Scripture tells of a man whose child was dead, yet when he went to the man of God and asked that the child be made alive once more, it was done unto him. Your ideal, be it for success, health, romance, money or fame, is your child who is dead. But if you will believe in its life and walk in the assumption that you are successful, healthy or wealthy (if that is your desire), your child which sleepeth will rise from the dead state and be made alive in your world.

The parable is told of a judge who it is said, "feared not God nor regarded man." Within you there is such a judge who will give you anything you ask for if you will be just as persistent as the widow in the story. Coming at the midnight hour, she persisted in her request until the judge granted her wishes saying, "Because this widow bothers me, I will vindicate her or she will wear me out by her continual coming." When the light of consciousness is not shining on your fulfilled desire, it is the midnight hour. But if you will fill your desire with your light of awareness and persist, then that which you are aware of, you will become.

You are forever surrounding yourself with the true image of yourself and what you are, that only can you see, whether it be good, bad or indifferent. Observe your reactions to life and you are observing the being you want to separate yourself from. And, as you begin to identify yourself with your chosen state, the separation takes place. But your assumption must be a maintained attitude and, if for a moment you lose the mood, recapture it. And if you lose it again, feel yourself back into the feeling until the mood becomes so natural your thinking from that mood is normal.

The great failure of most truth students is that they are perpetually constructing but deferring their occupancy. When entering your desired state, feel its presence surround you like an answered prayer. Then become so one with the state that your thoughts flow from it. Persist in viewing your world from that state, and it will harden into fact. You and you alone determine the time for the state to externalize itself. If your mind is so disciplined that it cannot be turned or diverted, your heart's desire will be outpictured on your screen of space. But, if you believe in any secondary power, your belief will cause its delay.

Your awareness is the power of the Word. It is divine, not divisional. There are not two I AM's but one I AM standing on many levels. Desire, claiming fulfillment now, wrestles as Jacob. But when the fight is over desire, as Israel, is born. You may think your name is John Brown or Mary Smith, but your real name is I AM and your dominant mood is your nature. Divorce a mood and assume a new nature. Persist in your new relationship and you will bear its children as new phenomena appear to bear witness to your creative inner I AMness. Only if you lack "importunity" and constantly return to the mood you are attempting to divorce yourself from, will failure occur. Desire is hidden identity. What you want, you already have! If you acknowledge, as fact, that you are already what you desire to be and will not be diverted but maintain your importunity by walking in the mood of fulfillment which now dominates you, no power on earth can keep you from expressing it. But you must feel yourself right into the situation of the answered prayer, for only by believing that you already have it, will it appear.

Anyone who prays successfully is, himself, the springboard of action and the one who grants the prayer. There is no other being to grant it. The one who receives the answered prayer is the one who grants it through the act of rearranging the mind. Learn to rearrange your mind and, if you find yourself walking in the field of unanswered prayers, turn around and walk in the field (mood) of fulfillment. And, remember, "Faith is the substance of things hoped for, the evidence of things not seen." The only reality and the only substance is consciousness from which all prayer has its beginning and its end.

The entire Book of Hebrews is devoted to faith: "Faith is enduring as seeing him who is invisible." And "Faith is the substance of things hoped for." "Unto us was this good news preached, as well as unto them, but it did not profit them because it was not mixed with faith." Good news is desire fulfilled. If desire is not mixed with faith, it is of no avail, for faith is the awareness of the reality of the desire's fulfillment. You see, creation is finished, and we only become aware of increasing portions of it. The absence of faith would be to deny the reality of the state assumed. If you limit yourself to your physical senses which contradict everything you desire, then faith will be unknown to you. But faith will make real that which is invisible.

The being you would like to be, though invisible, will unveil itself and become visible for all to see when you walk in the faith of its reality.

CHAPTER 7

Righteousness

If you have an objective and fail to achieve it you have sinned, for you have fallen short of your desire. But if you have no desire, you are incapable of sinning. The righteous man, however, being conscious of already having fulfilled his objective, cannot sin.

In the Book of Daniel we are told to "Break off your sin by righteousness." This has nothing to do with any church or ritual, for righteousness is right thinking. In the Book of Genesis the story is told of Jacob's desire to increase his wealth. Lifting his eyes in a dream he beheld the spotted lambs, the ring-striped goats and cattle. Then he said, "I will hold onto my righteousness and not let it go. So shall my righteousness answer for me in time to come."

Follow Jacob's example. Lift up your eyes with a controlled imagination and see what you want to see. Believe in your vision and your faith will make it solid and real in your manifested world. While sitting in your chair, you can assume the state of consciousness you desire to possess even though your reason and outer senses deny its reality. Then, as Jacob, you can say, "My righteousness shall answer for me in time to come." Jacob knew that he could not become perverse and turn from the new state but that if he maintained a consciousness of having what reason denied (including the law of genetics), he would achieve his goal.

God the Father is not a man, but the dominant idea that you serve. The enemies of that idea are those of your own household—your own thinking. Hold a dominant idea in your consciousness and, in a way you do not know your righteousness (right thinking) will cause the desired state to externalize itself in your world.

A Pharisee is one who conforms to all manmade laws; one who strictly observes the Levitical law of "outer purification." Now we are told, "Unless your righteousness exceeds that of the scribes and Pharisees, you will never enter the kingdom of heaven. But seek ye first the kingdom of heaven and its righteousness, and all these things shall be added unto you."

True righteousness is consciousness. We confuse the word and seek righteousness as a thing, but the consciousness of being is the magnet that draws a thing to it. Permeate your consciousness with the feeling of being the man (or woman) you want to be and your righteousness will bring it about.

You cannot inherit Christianity, rather you adopt it. As you come into its inner conviction, you become cleaner and more noble. Christ taught righteousness in his law of identical harvest saying, "As a man sows, so shall he reap." Taken psychologically, a state of consciousness sown within the mind, will be harvested without as external events. And, in like manner, as long as you remain sowing your present state of consciousness, you will continue to encounter similar events in your life.

Walk, conscious of the feeling that your wish is fulfilled, and you will never sin by missing the experience of fulfillment. But you cannot turn away and return to your former state. We are all the prodigal son who went astray. But we are told that when he came to his senses he turned around and entered his Father's house, at which time he was given the fatted calf, the robe, and the ring. When you observe who you are in consciousness and come to your senses by turning to your Father (the state desired), it will be given unto you.

Watch your reactions to life and you will discover where you stand psychologically. If your reactions are unlovely, you are walking in the mud and mire, feeding the swine. But when you turn within to the Father of all life and enter the state you desire by assuming its fulfillment, your actions will be lovely. Persist and you will move out of the mud and mire and enter the kingdom of the wish fulfilled.

There is no such thing as righteous indignation, for the wrath of man cannot work righteousness. Nothing so unlovely as righteous indignation could be right consciousness! My goal is to be one who expands in consciousness, for I am a teacher and I must ever grow as a teacher. This is my aim and I must remember it morning, noon and night. I must persist in this state as it externalizes itself in my world.

There is a story told of a little blind girl who had five brothers. The brothers, trusting their senses went out into the world and lost their way, while the little girl, unable to trust her senses wove a thread of gold. Attaching one end to her finger, she tied the other to the sun and never lost her way. You, too, can learn to trust the light of consciousness by holding onto the thread that is your aim and not allowing yourself to become enmeshed in the evidence of your senses.

Remembering your desire, you will not get lost like the five brothers as you will not be concerned with what others are doing, but simply walk conscious of being the one you want to be. No power can keep you from your goal when you are conscious of already having attained it.

You are told to, "Seek first the kingdom and its righteousness and all these things will be added unto you." The kingdom of heaven is within you. Turn within and you will find the power to produce what nature and your outer senses deny. Test yourself by controlling your thoughts, by seeing only what you want to see and hearing only that which contributes to the realization that your world is as you want it to be.

If you will keep controlling your world in your imagination until the one sensation crowds out all other ideas, your right consciousness will answer for you and your dream will become your reality. But, if you don't feel fulfilled, you can easily be diverted and miss your mark.

The Bible's teaching is one of rising higher and higher in consciousness until rebirth occurs. There is but one purpose in life, and that is to rise higher and higher on the vertical bar of the cross.

Knowing the state you desire to express, walk as though you are now expressing it. "No man, having put his hand to the plow, looks back." In other words, once you have moved into the new state, do not look back at the old state or you will become as Lot's wife. She looked back and was turned into a pillar of salt which is a preservative. The moment you look back at your former state, you re-enter it, as all states exist, preserved in your imagination and ready for occupancy.

The kingdom of heaven is a higher state of awareness; a step above where you now stand, and each higher level is reached by a change of attitude for the better. There is not a problem that cannot be resolved by a change of consciousness. And that which requires a state of awareness to produce its effect can never be effected without that state. It is the height of folly to expect security while being conscious of insecurity. On the other hand, you cannot be insecure if you walk conscious of being secure.

You don't have to "pull strings" to get what you want, all you need do is walk in the consciousness of already having it. For an assumption, though false, if persisted in, will harden into fact. Don't try to be a better man but try to be better at something. Most metaphysical students have no aim, claiming God knows best. But, I ask you, how can this be when you and God, your Father, are one? Human nature wants the thing to come first with belief to follow. But I say, you must assume the consciousness of already having (or being) your desire before the sign that you have it can appear. Signs follow; they do not precede. Seek the conscious feeling of having already reached your goal, and the sign that you have achieved it will follow. You don't get things and then become righteous; righteousness is right seeing. Always claim the level above the one you are now on by dying to your present level, for your Father's house has many mansions. Let go of your present mansion and reach for the one you seek!

CHAPTER 8

The Perfect Will of God

Understood psychologically, humanity is an infinite series of levels of awareness, and the individual is what he is according to where he is in the series. In the Book of Romans Paul urges us to: "Be not conformed to this world, but be transformed by the renewing of your mind that you may prove what is good and acceptable, the perfect will of God." In other words, do not look at the external world and call it reality, but break its spell by transforming your thinking. But you can't change your thinking until you change your ideas, for it is from ideas that you think. Remember, your level of awareness attracts life and is the sole cause of the phenomena you observe.

To be aware is to do the will of God whose name is I AM. Always being aware, what you are aware of is what you are. "I AM (aware of) that (which) I AM." Think of an infinite scale of values as I AM, with your desired state just above where you now stand. God speaks to you through the language of desire. When you wish to ascend, it is because God is speaking, calling upon you to surrender yourself to the feeling of already being what you want to be. Let go of fear, limitation and doubt and subject yourself to the will of God. A mere assumption will lift you up to the level upon which your ideal is identified, and you will begin to see your world differently. This is where self-observation comes in. You do not observe the outer world, but your reactions to it.

When another displeases or offends you, look within to the "I" who heard with displeasure and is expressing it. It is difficult to believe, I know, but you alone are the cause of your displeasure. A lady I know thought her employer was a monster and impossible to please. She had formed an opinion of him and that invisible and inaudible opinion spoke to her all day long, causing her boss to do what he did and say the words to cause her displeasure. Being a gracious lady and willing to change her feeling of "I", she heard her boss praise her and she thanked him for his praise. The moment she found herself returning to the old role of criticizing him, she stopped the thought and put on the new record of praise, thanks and congratulations. Within 24 hours, the new record externalized itself and, when she resigned a year later, her boss begged her to stay and told her that if she ever wanted to return, the door was always open to her.

Your inward conversations are the breeding ground of all your future action. Morning, noon and night you are carrying on internal arguments. When you catch yourself, break the habit by consciously creating new thoughts; thereby making a new record to externalize itself in your future.

God's will is I AM. His will is always being done, for it is the power which resurrects and makes alive. There is no transforming power in time, only transformation of the moment. If you are having difficulty with another, look into self, for it is the "I" called you who is speaking to you as a thought. Listen carefully to what you are saying to yourself and you will discover where the difficulty lies.

Let me now define "self" or "soul." It is that which you believe, feel, think and consent to. You may consent to the belief that you have been mistreated; that you are dumb, or they, in their cruelty, are causing your displeasure. If you do, your consent forms your level of being and attracts your life, be it good, bad or indifferent. Your soul cannot be changed by joining churches, synagogues or groups. You must turn to self, the inner "I" you know so well, as it is he who attracts those who mistreat you and determines every little detail of your outer experience.

If you have a secret affection for your conflicts, you cannot be helped. But, when you consent to be otherwise, then you can change. Subject yourself to the will of God by first knowing your ideal, then yielding to it by doing in your imagination what you would do physically if your desire were realized. Once this is clearly defined, repeat the act over and over again until you feel affected by it and its fulfillment possesses your mind. When the idea is so firmly entrenched and your thoughts flow freely from it watch, for you will have a change in your external world.

Become pure in heart by purging your mind from the belief in powers outside of yourself. Then, believing that consciousness is the only reality, weave yourself into a new state of awareness. For your world is your house, your state of consciousness externalized. Clean house by observing your thoughts. When you first begin to do this, you will discover most of your thoughts are unlovely. But, as you learn to passively think of people you dislike, your thoughts will lose their unloveliness and, with a mind filled with joy and thanksgiving you will ascend Jacob's ladder of self into the kingdom of love.

When you have carefully defined your desire, completely and utterly yield to it. Then try to remain faithful to the new idea you have entered. In the beginning you may not succeed, but don't condemn yourself. Simply return as many times as necessary until the feeling becomes so strong, your thoughts habitually flow from the new state.

This teaching is not for the weak. It is not for those who seek escape from life or want to point their finger of blame at another. To find the Christ in you who is your hope of glory, you must be willing to test yourself. I tell you, he is your "I" who calls all men and manifestations to you. Life is easier when you can blame another but I urge you to pray, not for an easy life but to become a stronger man. The one who is bearing witness to your thoughts is the cause of your misfortune, not the other fellow. Be transformed by the renewing of your mind and you will prove the good and acceptable word of God.

Would it be acceptable to you to be lifted on high? That is the will of God which will not turn back until he has executed and accomplished the intents of your mind. You are doing God's will when you identify yourself with your desire. And, if you believe your claim, you are righteous and your world will outpicture your righteousness. But if you do not believe you will miss your mark and die in your sins.

The only escape from the life you now lead is by a radical psychological transformation of self. This is done by defining your

"I" with your desire, then changing your thoughts until their effect possesses your mind and your "I" resides comfortably in the new state. Remember, your level of being attracts life, and unless the level changes your history remains the same. Let your present level die by subjecting your entire being to a level beyond it. Try it. It really is not difficult to do.

Remove the hold that past wrong emotional reactions have upon you by reviewing the experiences and changing them. This is done by rewriting the experience in your mind and saying what you should have said and doing what you should have done at the time. Let this corrected picture slip back into the subconscious as you resolve not to make the same mistake again. By repetition of this technique, you will rid yourself of all feelings of hate, resentment and other emotional disturbances which cling to your memory. And, to the degree that you release yourself from these destructive feelings, you will free yourself from their power to attract ill health and wrong results for you.

Relaxation of the body plus passivity of the mind and fixation of attention on the objective desire, equals fulfillment of the objective. Anxiety has no creative power. In this school of educative darkness, consciousness (whose origin is in eternity) provides the power for your experiences in time. So test yourself, for in this teaching there is no room for failure.

CHAPTER 9

Be Ye Doers of the Word

In the Book of Hebrews Paul tells us to "Rest in the Lord." Why? Because the man who rests in the Lord is transformed into the image in which he rests. If my aim is to be a good teacher and I rest in that feeling, I will be transformed into that image.

Unfortunately, most of the states in which men rest are negative. Feeling insecure, you will rest in the conviction that the world owes you a living. Feeling hurt, it is easy to rest in that grievance until your mood becomes natural. You may condemn the state and believe others to be its cause but, through your feelings of being hurt, you will be transformed into the very image of the state you condemn. And if someone seems to cause you displeasure, remember, there is no other. The state in which you rest is causing you to listen to silent and invisible conversations. Although the words are heard by you and you alone, they act as magnets and draw to you the circumstances of your life.

"Be ye doers of the word and not hearers only, deceiving yourselves." Every meeting I share with you the knowledge I have gained through personal experience, but I cannot make you put this knowledge into practice. As a teacher, I demand results. As a student, I urge you to test this truth, for if it is true it will prove itself in the testing.

In the 25th Chapter of the Book of Matthew the parable is told of the servants who were given talents by their master. One was given five talents which he increased to ten. Another, two talents were given which were increased to four. And when the third received his one talent he buried it, thereby never allowing it to increase. When the master returned, he rejoiced at the increase he was shown by the first two. But he took from the one who had placed his talent in hiding and gave it to the one who had ten, saying, "To everyone who has, more will be given and he will have abundance; but from him who has not, even that which he has will be taken away."

This teaching is like the talents. Practiced daily, your power of awareness will grow. If you are a hearer only, your knowledge, not used, will soon wither away and atrophy. Test yourself every day. Leave the other fellow alone and turn to self, for the promise is, "According to your work will it be done unto "

The man who overcomes himself, rises to a higher level of being. Uncritically observe your reactions to life, then work on yourself by practicing this psychologically. Only by working on self can you rise to a higher level. But you cannot do it with a negative emotion; it must be a positive one. We are told to "Lift up your eyes unto the hills from whence cometh your help." Negative thoughts cause downward emotions, while positive thoughts elevate. If you listen to your thoughts, stop their negative flow and change them so that you are hearing what you want to hear, you will feel a positive emotion of relief which is followed by a stillness that brings with it the knowledge that your prayer has been answered.

Now, as the title of this lesson implies, we are urged to be doers of the word and not hearers only, deceiving ourselves. In the Book of James, a hearer is defined as like a man who observes his natural face in the mirror, then turns and forgets what he looks like; whereas the doer is one who looks into the perfect law of liberty, perseveres, and is blessed in all that he does.

How do you go about looking into the mirror of the mind and being pleased with what you see? By looking into the face of your wife, husband, parent or friend. Close your eyes, relax and think of a friend who would rejoice in your good fortune. Tell him your good news and watch the expression of joy appear on his imagined face. His expression will liberate you, as his knowing has set you free to express your desire. Having looked into the perfect law of liberty, persevere and you will be blessed in the doing.

In the Book of Matthew the law is stated thus: "Whatever you wish that men would do to you, do so to them, for this is the law of the prophets." Here we discover that the Bible is speaking of a man's psychology and not his physical form. The Bible records what you do within yourself, telling you that the conversations carried on internally are the breeding grounds of your future actions. Forever carrying on mental conversations with imaginary beings, become aware of your thoughts. Be selective and make your inner conversations positive, for the mechanical imagination is asleep and negative, while the awakened imagination is positive and noble.

Tonight, single out someone you love and rearrange your opinion of him. Carry on mental conversations with him based upon this new premise and you are a doer of the word. If you don't, you are a hearer only, deceiving yourself.

This teaching is to awaken you to the active, dynamic being that you really are. Asleep, your thoughts are negative and passive and cannot change until you uncritically observe your reactions to life If you are honest with yourself, you will find an internal being you are not proud of, a monster that needs taming. Tame that monster by filling your mind with positive thoughts of joy and fulfillment, and you will turn that monster into a being of love.

Get into the habit of observing your reactions to life. Give yourself your daily bread by giving yourself the ability to no longer react negatively. Become a doer by recognizing a negative thought, then breaking it and going immediately to a positive one. All of your grievances, your hurts, self-pity and belief that others are the cause of your sorrow are animals which need to be sacrificed on the altar of consciousness. Letting all negative feelings go, select the mansion (state) you desire to enter and go in.

The law which brings poverty into being also brings wealth. Let the weak man say, "I am strong," and the poor man say, "I am rich," for only that which you affirm within yourself can be outpictured. Feel yourself into the state of poverty, and poverty is outpictured. Feel yourself into the state of security by saying, "I am secure," and security will result. But if you do not feel yourself into the state desired, you will be forever free of its results, as that which requires a state of consciousness to produce its effect will never be effected without such change in consciousness. You must feel yourself right into the situation of your answered prayer, then live and act in that conviction. If you don't, you will never know the results of that state.

Your fortune or misfortune was brought into being by your state of consciousness. There is no other cause. Have the courage to accept this and then become a doer and, in so doing be blessed in your every deed. Start now to become conscious of what you hear yourself say to yourself and stop receiving those impressions mechanically and unconsciously. What you hear must be filtered through what you are. And what you are is what you hear. Kind thoughts stem from kind ideas created by a kind person; therefore, be kind to one another, tenderhearted, forgiving each other.

Now, an assumption is called the crown of the mysteries and every assumption is made by you alone. The world you see depends, not so much on what is there, as on the assumption you make when you look at it. The talent entrusted to you is your power of conscious assumption. Don't bury it! Asleep to this knowledge, your reactions to the day are mechanical, negating everything you see and hear. Awake! Become conscious of what you are doing and saying to yourself, and rise in consciousness by controlling your thoughts and making them positive, kind, loving and fulfilling ones!

CHAPTER 10

The Pearl of Great Price

When you possess the mind of Christ, you are in possession of the p an of great price! That pearl is imminent. It is nearer than near and sooner than now, for the pearl of great price is your own wonderful human imagination. You have always possessed this mind but, like every possession, unless you know it is yours and are willing to use it, it is non-existent to you. Believe me, everything in your world was first conceived in your imagination. The house you live in, the car you drive, the clothes you wear, as well as your friends, your loved ones, your enemies and the strangers on the street were imagined before externalized. Now it is time to control your human imagination and govern it by love. I urge you to awaken to the discovery that everything you seek in time is contained within you.

There is only one mind with unnumbered levels of awareness. Your level determines where you are and what you are, for what you think, you are. This mind is not something detached from you but your own lovely imagination, the body of the Father and the only redemptive power in the universe. It can save you from your present state or bind you to it.

Christ is defined in scripture as the power of God and the wisdom of n you as your hope of glory. All things are made by this power without it is not anything made that is made, for Christ, who is your own wonderful human imagination, is yourself! Looking with the human eye, you see a world outside and seemingly independent of your perception. But when you view the world through the "I" of imagination, you understand its meaning. Turn within and test yourself and you will discover that you are your own savior. Then you will begin to assert the supremacy of your human imagination. You will cease to bow before the dictates of the world without and start to put your dreams into effect.

A tamed man is one who is self-disciplined. Tame yourself by observing yourself. Are you wasting your strength in negative emotions? If so, then discipline yourself out of the muck and mire you have been living in and rise, with your disciples, into a state of joy and the body of love. Do this, and you will have found the pearl of great price.

In this world, you appear to be a man (or woman) of flesh and blood. Your father, mother, sisters and brothers are known. But I tell you, you are far greater than the greatest man on earth, for you are Jesus Christ.

Imaginative love is sleeping in your body of flesh. Awaken the love that you are by claiming that your mind is Christ. Claim your pearl of great price, for it is the key that will unlock the treasure house of heaven. With your mind as Christ, you will discover that you are no longer capable of thinking unlovely, negative thoughts and will have no desire to retaliate.

The Bible is your biography, for you are Jesus, the great Jehovah of the Old Testament who finds fulfillment in the New. Using the mind of man, you are asleep. It is time to awaken, to cast off the mind of man who says, "I can," "I was," or "I will be," and assert your divine inheritance which is the mind of God who says, "I AM." Nothing is impossible to God, and nothing is impossible to you when you claim to be the mind of God.

This world is like a machine where its actions and reactions are automatic. Separate yourself from this machine-like mind and use your wonderful human imagination to rise to higher and higher levels of your own being.

If you do not like the events of your life, change them by controlling your imagination. When you know what you want, ask yourself where you would sleep if you had it. What would your world look like? Would a friend be happy for you?

With the answers to your questions filling your mind, fall asleep in your desired place.

View the world from that vantage point and hear your friend rejoice now that your desire is a physical fact. Then believe in Christ— the power to put all things under your subjection- and it will be done unto you.

Remember, there is no such thing as a powerful fate to which you must bow, nor do you have to accept life on the basis of the world without. Turn to self. Claim your pearl of great price and remember:

"What seems to be, is to those to whom It seems to be, and is productive of the most dreadful Consequences to those to whom it seems to be; Even of Torments, Despair and Eternal Death." for William Blake, in his poem Jerusalem, makes this promise: "...but Divine Mercy Steps beyond and redeems Man in the Body of Jesus."

CHAPTER 11
Self-Remembering

Do you have a goal in life? An aim for yourself? If you do, start now to lift yourself to its level by the act of self-remembering. Do not try to be a better man or woman, but transcend your present level of being by being better AT something. Your goal should be so important that you cannot forget it and your hunger for its externalization so intense that you cannot and will not let the thought go until it is embodied in flesh.

Scripture tells us, "Many are called, but few are chosen." The word "chosen" means to separate; to choose; to decide." Every day, you are offered the opportunity to choose a new idea; to enter a new state from which to think and feel. Unnumbered emotions and thoughts are yours to call forth but, because of the aim with which you desire to be identified, only a few emotions and thoughts are chosen. Begin to rise within yourself by letting go of your former beliefs and restrictions. Choose the thoughts and emotions you desire to express and enter your desire through the act of feeling.

In the 11th Chapter of Mark, two disciples were told to "Go into the village where you will find a colt tied at the crossroad upon which no one has sat. Loose him and bring him to me. If anyone says, 'Why are you doing this?' say, 'The Lord has need of him.' Then he mounted the unbridled ass and rode into the city of Jerusalem."

Now, the animal found at every crossroad is not a colt or ass but the individual's permanent, predominant emotion. Desiring to express a new emotion, you may find it difficult to ride. But you will always find your emotions tied at the crossroads of life. If you have never felt secure before, you may not be able to ride the animal emotion of security for more than a few seconds at a time. But the important thing is to try, for controlled imagination can ride any emotion into the city of Peace; the embodiment of the ideal state.

An emotion is right or wrong relative to a desire. If you feel uneasy as you commit yourself to your desire, you are walking in the wrong direction and will never reach it. But if the feeling is natural (right), and you persist in your assumption, it will become a fact. At times, even when your aim feels natural, you may allow doubts to creep in and move away from your goal. When this happens, don't condemn yourself, simply get back on that emotion and ride it again, for the beast is unbridled and must be ridden until you and it become one. Acknowledge the feeling of importance, of security, or of being dignified, within yourself, for your consciousness is reality. What you are conscious of being right now, you are. If you desire to be other than what you are remember, the state desired is just as real as the one you are conscious of now. Enter the new state by becoming conscious of being it. Persist! Find the feeling of the new state and ride it into Jerusalem.

Scripture calls upon man to remember himself by associating himself with his aim and walking in its direction. Only as you discipline yourself can you embody your aim. In his 11th Chapter Mark makes this statement, "Whatever you desire, believe that you have received it and you will. And whenever you stand praying, forgive." How do you fulfill a desire and forgive another? By finding the quality you thought to be in another and removing it from yourself. Then place the feeling you desire to express in its place. When this has been done, you have risen right into the state of your answered prayer.

Now, prayer is conditioned upon the belief that it is already answered. Desire is your springboard. Standing upon your desired state, you may discover that the board wobbles or the ground sways beneath your feet. But if you persist in being conscious of having attained your desire, even though your reason and outer senses deny it, what you are conscious of will become your reality.

Tonight, form a lovely aim for yourself and feel its fulfillment. Associate yourself with that feeling by becoming conscious of it. Do that and you will bless and be blessed by God who is your very self. Say to yourself, "I and my Father are one." Your inner being is he who men call God. He is never so far off as even to be near, for He is your own wonderful human consciousness.

All things, when admitted into your consciousness, are made manifest by its light, but something must be admitted first. If you are conscious of being beaten, the thought will manifest itself and you will be. Do you feel insecure? If you do, and persist in that mood you will sink into its slums, for everything manifested, is consciousness externalized.

What thought dominates your mind right now? Regardless of what it is, you have consented to it, but you need not perpetuate it. The thought which enters the mind does not defile you. You may consent to any thought, be it one that defiles or blesses you when it goes forth. But every thought will be made manifest. The state where you presently reside was only a thought before you entered it, just as is the state you now desire, and it can just as easily be realized. Take the challenge. Formulate your aim and rise, in consciousness to its fulfillment. Think it is real and it is, for everything is possible to a thought.

Self-remembering is remembering your aim so, in the course of a day you should ask yourself where you are psychologically. Your reality lives in a psychological country where you can walk in the mire, the valley, or the mountain tops. Choose this day the state you desire to enter. Feel its mood and acknowledge its fulfillment. Walk faithful to that assumption and, although your reason and your senses deny it, your persistence will cause it to become a fact.

You, all imagination, are the sum total of your reactions to life. This is the only cause and explanation of the events you encounter. If you do not like your world, change your reaction to it. Life will become easier when you are brutally frank with yourself and acknowledge your reactions to that which was created by you and is being reflected to you. Resolve to react only in a positive manner. Positive thoughts produce positive effects. As you see your world differently, your consciousness changes, thereby changing future events.

Your desire is always ready for incarnation. But as a desire alone it is incapable of birth. It must have human parentage. You are the human imagination scripture calls "Mary," as you are capable of conceiving an idea and giving it birth without the aid of any man. "Man" is called "the mold of God." Your I AMness is God the Father, and you, as Mary, conceive a desire of God. Locking your secret within yourself, walk faithful to your concept and you will bring forth its fruit.

Everyone is the Mary of the Bible. Her names means "water; the psychological truths of the mysteries."

Washing all literal concepts of the Bible from your mind, you are baptized and are born of water. Then, as you live faithful to your desire, you are the blessed Virgin, bearing that which is conceived by the Holy Ghost the holy desire.

CHAPTER 12
Your Destiny

Love is the only true power, and your power is in proportion to your love. When scripture speaks of the violent taking the kingdom by storm, it is not referring to violent characters, but the power of love which gives the force necessary to rise to a higher level of awareness.

There is no ultimate destiny for, understood psychologically, life is everlasting. It is the appeasement of a hunger whose main force is desire. Man rises on the springs of his desire, with every level of the vertical line of the cross within him so organized that it will lift him, through desire, to higher and higher levels of himself.

I, like all true teachers, teach the art of overcoming the violence that characterizes mankind's present level of being. In many ways, we have advanced beyond our forefathers, but we have remained just as violent as they. It is my wish for you that you break your violent, negative nature. For if you will, you will rise in consciousness and find your destiny waiting for you. Every moment in time you are offered the chance to prove your ability to overcome violence. How? By assuming that consciousness is the only reality and that nothing has reality save the consciousness you have of it. In that assumption, you will find the sole cause of the phenomena of life.

Your reactions to life define you, and as long as they remain as they are, your life will stay the same. Your world is but a projection of your state of awareness. Consciousness is the only substance and the only cause of the phenomena of life; therefore, it is impossible for change to occur until there is a change in consciousness.

All that you consent to, be it good, bad or indifferent, is projected into your world through your "I" of awareness. If security is your aim, you must establish an awareness of security so strong that you can feel it and say within yourself, "I am secure." You are free to consent to violence and grievances or security and peace of mind. Whatever you consent to by becoming aware of will be yours. Your aim is always just above the state where you now stand. Throughout the day, ask yourself if you are conscious of your aim, and you will discover how near or how far you are from it. If you are not conscious of being secure at the moment, claim that you are. Persist, and maybe tomorrow as you observe your day, you will find the awareness growing stronger and stronger.

Learn to stand alone by claiming, "I am what I am because I am conscious of being it." Stop looking at others and start observing your reactions to their behavior. Turn within and change your violent nature to one of love. Do that and you will ascend the ladder of life and reach your destiny. It is impossible to embody a new level of thought through the efforts of another. The rock upon which you must stand is consciousness. All other ground is sinking sand.

It is the height of folly to expect the incarnation of a new concept to come out of the evolutionary process. The thing you are seeking must be incarnated before it can be made visible. There is a wide difference between knowing something mentally and knowing it spiritually. I can teach you the law of identical harvest. You can read how to apply the law through my books and mentally know the steps necessary to have wealth, but you will never know wealth, spiritually, until you consciously say within yourself, "I am wealthy." A man is sick because he is conscious of being so. Let the sick man say, "I am well," the hungry man say, "I am full" and the troubled man say, "I am at peace," and their right consciousness will produce that which they are conscious of being. If you want to know what love is, you must become loving, for you cannot know a thing until you are it.

I am teaching the art of Being; the art of spiritually knowing a state. In the Book of Joel, we are told, "Let the weak man say, 'I am strong.'" This applies, not only to the physical body but to every facet of your being. Seek to know your desire spiritually, for only when the spirit feels the naturalness of the desire will it project itself in your outer world. Always remember, you will never experience what you refuse to affirm as true of yourself!

Awake! Become ever more aware of what is taking place within you. Lift up your cross and, without turning to the left or the right to ask another, turn within and consciously claim your aim, then watch it harden into fact.

If you do not apply my words, you remain right where you are, for you must be a doer in order to be blessed with your deeds. Desire is hidden identity, as you already are what you want to be. "Never would you have sought me had you not already found me." The level of being you seek can be found by changing your reactions to life to conform to the level you wish to express. It is not necessary to use pressure, pull strings or ask anyone to aid you.

All you need do is change your attitude. After clearly defining your aim, sincerely observe your inner conversations and your reactions with regard to it. When your thoughts and reactions are disciplined, your "I" will lift you to your higher level and fulfill your aim.

Your fellow man is not to be condemned, but awakened. This is done by awakening yourself. As you rise in consciousness, you take all men with you. Think of your wonderful human imagination as the vertical line of the cross, limitless, with time as the cross-section. You are free to ascend (or lift up) the cross, but you cannot rise until you deny your limitations. Christianity is a way of life. With your mental eyes wide open, adopt Christianity by becoming aware of what it is.

If you do not like what you are encountering in life, rearrange your thoughts by changing your consciousness. Form the state you desire and occupy it in your mind. This is how you transform self. As you yield to the state desired, watch your world. It will transform itself into the ideal held in consciousness.

Where you stand, the ground is holy, for you are the temple of the living God. Clear your mind of the trees of traditional thinking. Become pure in heart and you will see that consciousness is all and all is consciousness. You will discover that the state you are conscious of being is the state made manifest. No matter how reasoning justifies acts of violence, don't accept them. If you do, you contribute to the state and it is a state you do not want to experience.

The story is told of Jesus entering the temple and ridding it of the money lenders saying, "My house shall be called a house of prayer, but you have made it a den of thieves." This is not a material temple. You are the temple of the living God and the Bible is your biography. Thieves have taken over your house of prayer by placing false values there. Rid your mind of all beliefs of outside causes and reinstate the only true value of consciousness, the only true power of love.

CHAPTER 13
Your Personal Autobiography

The Bible, the most wonderful book in the world and the most misunderstood, is your personal autobiography. It is not the recording of historical events as your teachers teach, and its writings were never intended to be interpreted as such. The persons recorded there never existed, and the events never happened on earth. The Bible is speaking of the heaven within and the earth without.

Its story begins: "In the beginning, God created the heaven and the earth. And the earth was without form and void; and darkness was upon the face of the deep. Then the Spirit of God said, 'Let there be light' and there was light." The light spoken of here comes from heaven which is within you. The light which shines upon your earth is the light of your consciousness and shines from within you. The outer man (called the earth) is dark while the inner man (called heaven) is the being who was in the beginning with God and was God but is sound asleep. As your autobiography, the Bible tells how you are lifted up from your present level of being into a higher one.

In the Old Testament, we find the Pentateuch (the first five Books, as the law of Moses). These books were written in 500 B.C., while the earliest date known for the New Testament is 170 A.D. The first known New Testament did not include the Epistles to the Hebrews or the Books of Peter and James. (It is James who speaks of the double-minded man, declaring that he can receive nothing from the Lord.) Then we had the Apocrypha which consisted of early Christian writings that were excluded from the Jewish and Protestant Old Testament. These writings give four biographical sketches of a principle, rather than a man. It took nine hundred years for the Bible to come into its present form. So when you read it, always bear in mind that it is speaking of the kingdom of heaven within you. It is telling of a revelation of an eternal principle called Christ, who is your hope of glory. All of the characters recorded in scripture are aspects of your mind which you will discover as you fulfill your destiny, which is to fulfill scripture within yourself.

No man named Moses ever wrote any commandments on stones, rather the word "stone" means "literal truth." The literal minded man comes first and is given certain laws to live by, thus blocking psychological truth. As long as you see things on the outside as facts, your mind is blocked and you are unable to grasp their psychological meanings. But when you become thirsty for the truth and begin to apply the law, the spirit of God will move upon this psychological sea of understanding and your life will take that truth (water) and turn it into wine. In the state of Moses, God's true name is revealed to you. Take his name (your I AM) as your rod of understanding and hit the stone of literal truth with it, and psychological water will come forth. Drink it by putting my words into practice and you will convert the psychological water of truth I have given you into the wine of the spirit.

Now, the clothing spoken of in scripture is that of the mind and not of the body. John the Baptist is described in the 3rd Chapter of Matthew as one called Elijah in 2nd Kings. It is said he wore a garment of camel's hair and a leather girdle around his waist. Hair and skin are the most external things a man possesses; therefore, John the Baptist represents the outer man who has not yet clothed himself internally. Jesus is the inner man. He wears the seamless g8rment woven from above, and those who wear his garment are always found in the king's house.

The New Testament teaches a complete and radical transformation of self and calls it rebirth, but John the Baptist calls it repentance and urges us to change our thinking of the kingdom of heaven. It is said that he lived in the wilderness with the wild animals. Well, you are John, living in the wilderness when you have no direction of your own and allow your animal emotions to run wild. But when you begin to tame your animal instincts and call them into discipleship, strength will come to you from within and you will be baptized in the water of truth.

Speaking in a parable, Matthew likens the kingdom of heaven to a sower who sows his seeds on different types of soil. The sower spoken of here is not a being external to yourself, for you are the sower and the seed. Your own wonderful human imagination is God, the sower who said, "Let us make man in our image," then fell asleep and annexed the brain of the outer man as the seed for his redemption. As Adam (or the red earth), man is the psychological earth upon which the kingdom of heaven is planted. In the parable, we are told that when one hears the word but does not understand it, the evil one comes and snatches away that which is sown in his heart. But he who hears with understanding, bears fruit and yields a hundredfold.

Another parable is told comparing the kingdom of heaven to a man who, having sowed good seeds in his field, fell asleep and his enemy came and sowed weeds there. These weeds are false teachings, planted in the mind, false beliefs and concepts that can be bound and burned when you turn within to discover the truth and the kingdom of heaven to be yourself.

In the 11th Chapter of Genesis, the story is told of how the tower of Babel is built with stone (literal truth) and bricks (manmade concepts). Before the building was erected, there was only one language and few words, but during the building, confusion reigned, and soon no one understood the language of the other. This tower exits today as the little mystical, occult groups of the world. You have no enemies save those of your own household. Making truth of false teachings, you believe that your security depends upon the money you have in the bank; or your health depends upon the pills you take; or your happiness depends upon another. In so doing, you build your own tower of Babel. But I say to you, your consciousness of being is the only reality of the state you are in, and all of the enemies of that state are within you. In his Beatitudes, Matthew tells you that your attitude of being is blessed when it is clothed in soft raiment, for when you wear the seamless garment of imagination, you are free to rise higher and higher into the garden of Eden within you. You are the gardener of your mind where you plant the seeds of your own selection. As the Man of Imagination, become conscious of being that which you have planted, and your harvest will be an hundredfold, for you always become what you behold.

In his 16th Chapter, Matthew tells the story of the Pharisees and Sadducees who, unbelieving, ask for a sign from the heaven. Then we are told to take heed and beware of the leaven of the Pharisees and Sadducees. Now, these are not men, but attitudes of mind. If you believe that you must live in the "right" neighborhood; that you must know the "right" people that your skin must be the "right" color; or that you must be in the "right" place at the "right" time, your attitude is one scripture calls a Pharisee. Beware of that kind of thinking, for the road to a higher level of self is always internal and never external.

Mark tells us that the kingdom of heaven is like a merchant of fine pearls who finds a pearl of great price, sells all that he has, and buys it. As long as you hold onto one thought of something external to your own mind, you do not have enough money to buy the pearl of great price. You must be willing to sell all belief in anything outside of self. The road to the kingdom leads upwards and is always in an internal direction. You cannot travel this road wearing clothes made of skin and hair. You must be clothed in your wedding garment which is always woven from within.

Again, we are told that the kingdom of heaven is like a net which is cast into the sea and gathers fish of every kind, be they good or bad. When it is brought ashore, the good are placed into vessels and the bad thrown away. Become discriminating. Select your thoughts carefully and throw away any unlovely and negative ones. Allow only that which is of good report to fill your mind and you will be the good fisherman. In this same 13th Chapter of Matthew, the question is asked, "Have you understood this?" It is my prayer that everyone of you will answer, as they did to him, and say, "Yes." Now it is said, "Do not put new wine into old wineskins, for the skins will burst and the wine be spilled, and the skins destroyed; but put new wine into fresh wineskins so both are preserved." Old thoughts, the traditions of men, the belief in power outside of self are the old wineskins which must be burst and allow the beliefs to be spilled and destroyed. New wine, gained by the fulfillment of God's promise within, must be put into your consciousness (fresh wineskins) so that both are preserved.

Man does not evolve on the outside. There is only one presence; only one essence in man, called Christ and defined as God's power and your hope of glory. This power can be awakened if you, God's word, are not tarnished by the belief in a power outside of self. Awake! Give up all false beliefs and clothe yourself in the soft raiment of an internal attitude which implies the fulfillment of your dream. The Bible, from beginning to end, is the psychological story of your soul and tells you that the first thing you must do is change your thinking. I bring to you a new idea relative to the cause of the phenomena of life, telling you that you are not what you believe yourself to be, but possess possibilities of infinite inner growth.

Your destination is always reached by an internal direction, which is the Be-attitudes. Be your attitude good, bad or indifferent, when you clothe yourself in an attitude, its fulfillment is not dependent upon anything external to you. But when you depend upon external laws to determine your attitude, you are on the level of Elijah and John the Baptist. Their teaching was wonderful, but it was stone, and the state was a violent one. John the Baptist cannot enter the kingdom of heaven. You must overcome his state by consciously turning within and disciplining your internal attitudes. This is your destiny. You are destined to awaken within yourself as you climb Jacob's ladder of states to higher and higher levels of your own being. The state of awareness you desire to express must be bought by selling all of your beliefs in any external power to help you. Once free from their encumbrance, you will move in faith into your desired state.

In the Book of John, Jesus, as a teacher, makes this statement: "Let not your heart be troubled; you believe in God; believe also in me." Then he adds this thought: "It is expedient that I go, lest the comforter will not come." Here we see a teaching that is seemingly taught from without, but it is necessary for your belief in any external teacher to disappear for only then can the comforter within you be found. As your belief in yourself grows, your heart will find peace.

There is only one cause, only one I AM. I, the trinity, in unthinkable origin, AM God the Father, and in creative expression AM the son, for imagination is born of consciousness. I, in universal interpretation; in infinite imminence; in eternal procession AM God, the Holy Spirit. The real definition of imminence is "sooner than now and nearer than here." I AM, therefore, the comforter. What could comfort you more than the knowledge that you don't have to wait for your dreams to come true? They are nearer than here and sooner than now. Let this knowledge be your comforter. If there was a limit to that which is contained in an infinite state, it would not be infinite. In the 23rd Chapter of Exodus, this statement is made: "You shall not steep a kid in its mother's milk." I tell you, you are doing this very thing when you keep your mind on a negative state. Turn your attention from want and lack (all negative states) and place it on fulfillment and abundance (positive states) and you will no longer simmer your desire in its mother's milk.

CHAPTER 14

The Human Spirit

The Bible tells of the human spirit's never-ending struggle to assert its supremacy over the natural mind. Believing in the reality of the world outside, the natural mind rules sleeping man, while the human spirit is God in man, struggling to awaken and assert its supremacy over all. The poet Faust knew this when he said, "Two souls are housed within my breast. One to heaven doth aspire and the other to earth doth cling." In the 25th Chapter of Genesis this struggle is told as the story of Isaac's two sons, Esau and Jacob. Coming first as outer skin and hair, Esau is recognized as your personality, while the smooth-skinned Jacob is your human spirit. We are told that when their mother Rebekah became aware of the struggle within her, she questioned the Lord who told her, "Two nations are in your womb and two people born of you shall be divided. One shall be stronger than the other and the elder shall serve the younger.

Your external world is known by reason of your critical faculties; therefore, you can always discover the psychological state in which you reside by observing your thoughts of the day. Now, every state has its limitations and restrictions from which there appears to be no escape. If you believe you are the state in which you now reside, you will never be able to leave it. But the story of Esau and Jacob tells you there is a way of escape and how to accomplish it.

Esau exists in your mind as the outer world of fact and Jacob as the inner world of imagination. As their father, you have the power to give either son the right of birth. Always seeing from where you have placed your attention, you are called upon to blind yourself to the outside world by drawing your attention from it, then deceiving yourself by imagining the world as you want it to be. This is done by closing your eyes to the so-called "facts" of life and turning your thoughts inward. Now, clothe your thoughts in the feeling of reality until they are just as solid and factual as those known to you by reason of your outer senses. When this is done you, Isaac, have given your son Jacob the right of birth.

Your objective world is always reflecting your inner, subjective state. Therefore, it is impossible to change your outer world until you have changed your inner, subjective state. Knowing the state you want to occupy, completely absorb yourself in it as though it were a sponge and you the water capable of entering and being absorbed by it. So lose yourself in the feeling of satisfaction and fulfillment that when you open your eyes and Esau (the world without) returns, you know you have given his birthright away. Although you have been self-deceived by imagining the state to be real, you have given it the power to be born. How it is going to come about I do not know. Only your Father in heaven knows, for he has ways to make your desired state alive and His ways are past finding out.

Now, there is an essence in you that is sound asleep and must be awakened. When you give Jacob the power you have given Esau, watch. You will discover that Esau will no longer react violently but will become passive. Then you will know that you have brought about a reversal of order. As you are aware of being Jacob, you will persist in seeing what you want to see and experiencing what you want to express, thereby awakening your true essence to the truth that the world is yours and all within it.

You are the Rebekah the Bible tells about and you are constantly bringing forth your Esau and your Jacob who are forever at war with one another. The elder is the world you know by reason of your critical faculties, while the younger is the one you know subjectively. The person you want to be is struggling for birth. As long as you look at and accept the outer world as the only reality, you will never give birth to your fulfilled desire. You must turn your attention inward and subjectively appropriate your objective reality.

When you read the 25th and 27th Chapters of Genesis, remember, all the characters recorded there are in your mind. Although unmarried, you are always giving birth to twins. The world in which you live is the outpicturing of your state of awareness. That state is your first son which must be supplanted by your second son, or desired state. Throughout the Bible, you will find there is always a second son which replaces the first: Jacob supplants Esau; Jesus supplants John the Baptist; and the human spirit supplants human matter.

When you know what you want, define it as vividly as you can. Then blind yourself to your externalized state by sending it hunting. You cannot touch your second son (your cherished idea) until you do. This is accomplished by turning your attention away from all thoughts of denial and clothing your desire with the skins of reality. In his "Ode to a Nightingale," Keats said:

"My heart aches, and a drowsy numbness pains my sense as Though of hemlock I have drunk."

Having felt the reality of his experience so vividly, when he opened his eyes, Keats asked:

"Was it a vision, or a waking dream? Fled is that music: do I wake or sleep?"

It is with this kind of intensity that I would ask you to clothe yourself as you feel yourself already the person you want to be. Now, stretch out your imaginary hands and touch the objects there. Listen with your imaginary ears. See with your imaginary eyes. Walk in your imaginary world as you taste and smell the objects there. Your creative power can be used for anything, be it a fur coat or a new hat. It is my hope that you will use it for some noble state such as greatness in your chosen profession, whatever that may be. Now, let us look at the 38th Chapter of Genesis where the story of Judah and Tamar is told. "Judah" means "praise" and "Tamar" means "a desired state; a palm tree oasis. As Tamar, you thirst for your desire. Give it to yourself by going into your desired state and making it real by becoming one with it. Feel the sense of satisfaction that your prayer has been answered and you are the woman called Tamar and the man named Judah.

You will find another account of twins in the 48th Chapter of Genesis. This is the story of Manasseh (which means to forgive) and his brother Ephraim (which means to affirm). One is negation and the other affirmation. When you take your attention away from your problem by affirming its solution, the problem is momentarily forgotten. Persist in your affirmation, not in repetitious form, but in feeling. As you feel the solution, the problem dies from lack of attention.

This teaching is not for the complacent but for the human spirit who hungers and thirsts after right thinking. As we are told in the 5th Chapter of Matthew, "Blessed are those who hunger and thirst after righteousness, for they shall be satisfied." Awaken the Jacob in you by observing your thoughts uncritically. Think of yourself as two beings, one who sees with the organs of sense and the other who sees through the mind of imagination. The sense man is a creature of habit. He is dynamic and active; yet, through the daily practice of self-observation, he can be brought into a passive state and his power transferred to the man of imagination. There are always two decided outlooks on the same world, i.e., the one you see with your outer organs and the one you know only mentally. Your desire is mental, without shape or form. It is your second son who will supplant your present world when your power of awareness is turned within.

Do you have a longing? A consuming desire that you want fulfilled now? Allow that desire to clothe your mind. Knowing that its fulfillment is based upon feeling, ask yourself what the feeling would be like if your desire were now realized. Whatever your problem is, its solution is within you. Turn your attention to your desire's fulfillment and clothe it in the skins of objective reality. This is the technique of reversal and should never be taken lightly because the moment you feel yourself into a state, you instantly take upon yourself the fruit of that state.

I hope you now know how to clothe your subjective longing. Think of your desire as Jacob; then clothe it in the skins and hair of Esau. The time it takes for your longing to materialize is proportionate to your feeling of its naturalness.

The kingdom of heaven is within you. Humanity cannot enter this kingdom, but your imagination can when you detach yourself from that to which you are now attached. There must be a separation, for only the human spirit is called, and only the human spirit can pass, singly, through this "I."

Now, that which requires a state of consciousness to produce its effect cannot be effected without such a state. Once you have entered a state, don't be concerned as to how it will be externalized, for everything comes into being through consciousness. You never create a state. All states were created before the world was. Rather, you enter a state and it simply displays itself. Enter the state of poverty by saying, "I am poor" and you will see its evidence displayed on your screen of space. You do not generate health, wealth or happiness. The states are already there, completely furnished and ready for your immediate occupancy.

My words are true, but truth by itself can do nothing. It must be applied. Unapplied truth is like a lamp without oil, but applied truth is a lamp whose oil never runs low. Remember, there are no accidents, no cause other than an imaginal one. If an accident is fatal, it is an involuntary suicide. Are we not told, "No one takes my life, I lay it down myself. I have the power to lay it down and the power to take it up again." An accident is not a force external to the individual's consciousness. "No one knows a man but the spirit of the man who dwells in him," and man is simply the sum total of his reactions to life. No one comes into your world save you call him. You have the power to call anything into being, for you are the author of the drama called life.

The Bible refers to God as the Father; as I AMness, or light, but the word means consciousness" which, like an atom, has no age. consciousness is living substance which has no beginning and no end but simply displays arrangements of itself. External man consents to age, but the substance of consciousness does not. It never changes. Before the world was, I AM, and when it ceases to be, there will still be I AM. External man can say "I was" or "I will be," but the internal human spirit says only "I AM." Knowing your desire, persist in the thought that you already have it until your thoughts become habitual. If you do not, you will find yourself returning to your old way of thinking and perpetuate it, thereby never seeing your desire externalize itself.

I will leave you with this thought. While man is violent, animals must exist. The animal is only externalized evidence of man's violence. The dinosaurs were lumbering beasts with small brains and bore witness to the lumbering state of man at that time. The dinosaurs were not killed off but became extinct naturally. Let man become tame and all the animals will become sterile.

CHAPTER 15

The Feeling of "I"

Your journey into this world of decay and death began with your feeling of "I" and where you place that feeling, there you live. You can place your feeling of "I" in the mud of negation or on the lovely ground of positive assumption. Your feeling of "I" is always with you. It is your slave and your savior, for wherever you go, there "I" am also.

The 9th Chapter of Numbers begins with Moses being given instructions by the Lord as to how to erect a tabernacle, or tent of testimony and move it across the desert. He was told: "During the day a cloud will cover the tabernacle, and at night it will have the appearance of a pillar of fire. Whenever the cloud rises, the children of Israel must journey to the place where the cloud settles down, there the people must remain. It may rise once a week, once a month, or longer, but when it ascends, the children of Israel must journey."

Now, a tabernacle is an elongated place of worship which is movable and covered with skin. You are that temple (tabernacle), and the spirit of God dwells within you as your "I." A cloud is a garment of water (or psychological truth) which covers the "I" and that to which it testifies. The cloud does not move in time but is lifted up by the "I" it covers. According to my senses, "I" am now in the Palace Hotel. Let me lift the cloud from my testament by withdrawing the feeling of "I" from the evidence of my senses and move by placing my "I" in a predetermined state, and my whole world moves with me. Clothing myself in feeling, the cloud covers me as I testify to the state I have just entered. At this moment, you may have placed your feeling of "I" in an unlovely state and, unless you lift that cloud which covers you, you are anchored there and are incapable of changing the circumstances of your life. Now, this lifting of the cloud and placing your feeling of "I" in a more desirable state involves a death, for when the cloud rises, it breaks (or kills) the cycle of recurrence you have been on.

Motion can be detected only as a change of position with respect to another body, and all motion spoken of in scripture is psychological. Every state exists in this psychological land from which your "I" journeys. All you need do is extract your "I" from where it is now and place it in your predetermined state. But how will you know you have moved? By using a frame of reference. While sitting quietly in your chair, you can lift your cloud by placing the feeling of "IF" in an entirely different psychological state. No one can see this motion, for yours is a spiritual journey. While in the state, look for confirmation of your move on the faces of people there. Are they surprised to see you? Are they happy for you? A little jealous? Look, until you see the expressions on their faces. If there is a change in your feeling of "I," you will find an automatic alteration in your usual expression of life.

During the day, you wear your garment of truth (the cloud); but the moment you begin to meditate, the brain grows luminous. This is the pillar of fire by night. Remember, "I AM the truth," and wherever you place your feeling of "I," there you must abide.

In the 34th Chapter of Deuteronomy we are told that Moses went up from the plains of Moab to Nebo, and there to Pisgah which is opposite Jericho, where he was shown all the land that was his. The word "Moses" means "to draw out." He is not a man but your creative power which can draw out of you any state you have placed your "I," struck the rock, and produced the water.

The word "Moab" means "mother/father" which is your "I AMness." In your present state, your Moab may be saying, "I am beaten," "I am sick," "I am impoverished." But "Nebo" means "to prophesy your longing by the feeling of I." "Pisgah" means "to contemplate." When you enter your desired state, observe your Jericho, for it will have a fragrant odor as that is what the word "Jericho" means. Having risen in consciousness, remain in your chosen state until you have a reaction that satisfies you. A violent reaction produces a horrible odor, while a lovely reaction indicates Jericho and a lovely odor. You see, Jericho is not a place in the Near East, but a state which produces the thrill of accomplishment within you.

In the 14th Chapter of the Book of John, Jesus speaks to Peter saying, "Let not your heart be troubled; you believe in God, believe also in me. In my Father's house are many rooms; if it were not so would I have told you that I go to prepare a place for you? And when I go and prepare a place for you I will come again and take you to myself that where I am, you may be also." This is not a man speaking to another, but self speaking to self. You are Jesus (Imagination) telling yourself that there are unnumbered states of awareness for you to enter, and you are inviting self to choose the state you wish to inhabit. After selecting the state, imagination will go and prepare it for you so that you may come again (as you must), for wherever you abide in imagination, there you shall reside also in the flesh. If you believe what I have told you, determine to change your feeling of "I." There is no power that can keep you from realizing your dream, but you! And no man can compel you to enter any state. You have the power to select your state and enter it, thereby making it alive or, leave a state, thereby killing it. The decision (and its consequences) is yours and yours alone. The day you can become an observing "I," watching your reactions and seeing the observer and the thing observed as two distinct beings, you will know you can enter any state and it will outpicture itself. You will know that all the mansions of your Father's house are yours.

I AM (consciousness) contains the whole of creation, and out of I AMness comes imagination. Where there is no consciousness, there is no imagination. When you enter a state, your I AM is having a psychological experience. When you think about a state, you have a subject and its object; but when you experience a state, you have unification.

Tonight, mentally look at your day. Can you remember those you saw this morning? If your reaction to them is the same as it was earlier, then you have not changed your feeling of "I." Your friends and relations are your frame of reference. Use them in your journey. The command in the 1st Chapter of Joshua is: "When you start, turn not from it to the right hand or to the left that you may prosper wherever you go, for I, the Lord your God, am with you." Therefore abide in the state you desire until your whole being is permeated with its reaction that you may reap its reward. "I," your consciousness, am with you, and I AM the Lord, your God.

The teaching of truth deals with the feeling of "I," for only through feeling can change come about. If you continue to have the same reactions, you have not changed your feelings. Your world forever conforms to your inner assumption. Remember your aim a thousand times in the course of a day. Notice your thoughts in regard to it, and break all unlovely ones. If you are not successful, it is because you not practicing this truth and applying this law.

"You are the temple of the living God, and the Spirit of God dwells in you. What has a believer in common with a non-believer? Come out from them and separate yourself from them, and I will welcome you." Come, let us live on the mountaintop!

CHAPTER 16

The Wine of Eternity

The human imagination and Divine Imagination are one and the same. They are not two. Your human imagination has the power to turn your water of life into the wine of eternity. This you will do when you release your imagination from its bonds of limitation, for when imagination is truly free, it can accomplish miracles.

The Bible calls imagination man's savior and identifies this wonderful benefactor as Christ. When Christ is awakened and born in you, your human imagination becomes divine vision. Called Christ, your individual imagination is the mediator between the father of all life and the external world called Man. Having imagined wealth, it is the human imagination who walks on the water of life and denies the evidence of his senses by claiming, "I am wealthy." His persistence mediates God to Man.

Every character in scripture lives in the mind. When you read the Bible, turn to self and ask, "What state would I be in if I were doing this?" When reading the story of Moses, claim you are he. Assume the state of faith when you read of Abraham. You are Joseph, the dreamer, and Thomas, the doubter; and you are destined to be Jesus Christ, the awakened, Risen Imagination.

Skin is the most external thing a man can wear. When you read of one who wears camel's hair or leather, you are reading of one whose mind is tied to the outside. His philosophy of life is external and dependent entirely on others. In the 5th Chapter of Mark, the story is told of an innocent man who, being unclothed, lived among the dead and cut himself on the stones. When Awakened Imagination passed by, the innocent one cried out, "Do not cast me out," and when asked his name, he answered, "My name is Legion, for we are many." A being not yet individualized in a spiritual sense is innocent for he knows not what he is doing. He is Legion because he has innumerable "I's" in him, i.e., "I am ill," "I am poor," "I am tired," "I am weak," and "I am mistreated," to name but a few. Living among the dead and sleeping the sleep of death, his literal understanding of life and its cause are stones which cut and bruise. But the spiritual man has a personal self-determined history, a predetermined self. In the realm of the spirit, he becomes what he wills. When consciousness turns within, the spirit awakens to his true identity. Then, casting out all belief in any external cause, he is clothed in his right mind and sits at the foot of the one who cast them out.

A miracle is only the name given by those who have no faith in the works of faith. The story is told of a man named Jairus whose daughter was believed to be dead. But Awakened Imagination ignored the thought and said, "Do not fear, only believe." Arriving at the house, he questioned, "Why do you weep? The child is not dead, but sleeping." Then he touched the child and said, "I say to you, ~rise." Immediately, she got up and walked. Then Jesus turned to the parents and said, "Give her something to eat." Every state, every desire, every idea is your child. Looking at the desire, it appears to be dead to you, the natural man. But your spiritual "I" knows the desire is not dead but sleeping, waiting to be touched for its resurrection. With your desire, (child) made alive within you through the power of touch, it must be fed in order to bring about its birth. This is done by turning your attention to it.

Now let us turn to the 5th Chapter of the Book of John where he speaks of the pool of Bethesda and its five porches. The story is told of a sick man who waits for the moving of the water by an angel, believing that whoever steps into the pool first, after the movement, will be healed. After asking him if he wanted to be healed, Awakened Imagination said, "Rise, take up your pallet and walk," and at once the man was healed and, taking up his pallet, he walked away.

The word "Bethesda" means "house of mercy." And the pool spoken of here is consciousness which must be stirred by an angel (a messenger of God). Any idea you entertain is that angel, disturbing your consciousness. The pool is entered by a mere assumption, and stirred as you bathe in it. "I am" is always first person, present tense. No one can put you in the pool by affirmation. Although seemingly impotent, you rest on the five porches, or senses when you accept their evidence and refuse to change your consciousness. No one need help you. Who could be first in the pool other than self which is your "I." Knowing what you want, rise in the assumption that your desire is already satisfied (healed) and it will be.

In his 17th Chapter, John rejoices saying, "I have finished the work thou gayest me to do. Father, glorify thou me in thine own self with the glory which I had with thee before that the world was. I have kept them in thy name which thou hast given me and none is lost but the son of perdition. For their sake, I consecrate myself that they also may be consecrated in the truth, for I dwell in them and they dwell in me and we are one." The work you gave yourself to do is to awaken from this dream of life. Having assumed the limitations of the flesh, you will awaken to your true identity and become your own glory when the outer you is made passive and the inner you, dynamic. Now, the son of perdition is the belief in loss. Knowing that all things exist in the human imagination, nothing can be lost. When you realize this truth, you will no longer believe in loss, thereby fulfilling scripture.

The most difficult thing to grasp is that there is no one outside of self. Believing others needed to change, I worked on them, thinking that the world would be so much better if they would be different. Then I awoke and sanctified myself, and in so doing, they were sanctified, for I dwell in them and they dwell in me and we are one. There is no one to change but self. As you control your thoughts and allow only those which conform to your ideal to flow from you, your world will reshape itself in harmony with them. Remember, you cannot be aware of a fault or greatness in another were that fault or greatness not present in you. Remove the fault from your own "I". Place the greatness there and watch your world change as it reflects your change in consciousness.

In the 16th Chapter of Matthew, the disciples were questioned, "Who do men say the son of man is?" They said, "Some say John the l3aptist, others Elijah, and others Jeremiah, or one of the prophets." Then he asked, "But who do you say that

I AM?" Simon Peter replied, "You are the Christ, the Son of the living God."

At the present time, you may be concerned as to what others think of you, but when you have awakened to your true divinity, it will not matter to you what others think. You will know from experience that you are the Christ, the Son of the living God. Flesh and blood will not reveal this to you, but your Father who is in heaven reveals it. Through this knowledge, you will have been given the keys to the kingdom, and whatever you bind on earth will be bound in heaven, and whatever you loose on earth will be loosed in heaven. Having found the answer to the everlasting question, "Who am I," no man can ever take this knowledge from you. This wisdom comes from within.

Completely abandon yourself to a psychological experience. If you become one with a state in your imagination, you will rise to e compass it in the flesh. This being true, yours is a journey from innocence to imagination to experience.

You are already the person you want to be. Claim it and tomorrow y u will display it by being it. By your fruits you shall be known.

If today your life is not what you want it to be, stop blaming anyone; just keep working on changing your feeling of "I" and abide in your desired state. Persist...persist...persist, for at the moment of non-reaction, circumstances change. We rise by an energy others call effort, for it takes energy to act and react. All through the day, remember your aim by constantly identifying yourself with it. Let your reactions flow into your aim. Ask for deeper and deeper understanding of that which you think you now understand. I trust everyone has an aim to be greater. Do not limit yourself to any textbook. Stop believing that any one man can write a book that is final regarding truth. Start to dig. No one can grow without outgrowing. A different attitude is the solution to every problem. By your new direction (attitude) you escape that which has been wrapped around you. There is no one to change but self, so start changing yourself today!

Luke was speaking of you when he made this statement, "When their eyes were opened, they recognized him and he vanished from their sight."

When your "I" is awakened, you will find that which you have been searching for, and the belief in a power outside of self will disappear. In Francis Thompson's poem, The Hound of Heaven, he tells of how: "I fled Him, down the nights and down the days; I fled Him, down the arches of the years; I fled Him, down the labyrinthine ways Of my own mind..."

only to discover at the end that "He was my very self."

Man's eyes are blind, though hounded constantly by the Hound of Heaven. He cannot believe in the non-historicity of the Bible but continues to hold onto his little beliefs even though he does not know what to do with them. People do not seek truth; they seek only supports for their opinions of it. But I say to you, "Do not think that I have come to bring peace on earth; I have not come to bring peace, but a sword. I have come to set a man against his father and a daughter against her mother and a daughter-in-law against her mother-in-law, for a man's foes are those of his own household." When truth comes, it sets a man at war with himself, for he will discover that he can no longer consent to what he formerly believed in.

Start now and quietly listen to the words you want to hear. By a new direction, internally, you can change the course of your life and free yourself from the prisons of your mind. You can see yourself best by looking into the face of another, but you cannot judge one who has not awakened from the dream of life. Living in his physical, animal world, he reacts mechanically and automatically just like a machine.

CHAPTER 17

Awake, O Sleeper

In the Book of Ephesians we are told to "Awake, O sleeper, and arise from the dead, and Christ shall give you light." This awakening and rising comes about through an inner development, for the Bible is your autobiography. It was you who inspired the prophets to record their visions. And it is you who will fulfill their prophecies in a first person, present tense experience. As you read the Bible, get your mental teeth into it. Study its message, and your understanding will go deeper and deeper as you travel through life.

The Bible teaches self-help. Do not look to any leader on the outside, only look to self by turning within. If anyone offers to do for you what you can do for yourself, reject their offer and turn to Christ, God's creative power in you, who is your life, your light of the world. By changing your thinking, Christ will change your world.

The "earth," spoken of in scripture, is the "mind of man." It is in this psychological earth that the idea of the kingdom of heaven was implanted. While in the state of sleep, false doctrines have crept in. Called tares, they grow with the wheat and will be harvested; therefore, you must become selective and clear the weeds by killing every belief in a power outside the mind.

The man who is rich is complacent. Satisfied with his social and financial positions, he is not hungry to grow. If you are complacent, your life will not change, for you will not be hungry or thirst for a higher level of awareness. You and you alone know whether the hunger has come upon you or not; but you have not begun the work you gave yourself to do until you begin to uncritically observe your thoughts. And when you do, you will discover that you are not as truthful, honest, or courageous as you thought you were.

Tonight, select a future upon which you want to work and tomorrow, be watchful. Question yourself by saying, "Am I keeping the tense? Do I want this? Is that the way my friend wants me to see him? Am I limiting myself?" Then act in your imagination, for imagination is passive while asleep and allows that which is false to take the throne. Watch your thoughts. Reclaim your throne and consciously allow your human imagination to rule your world! Your human imagination, once activated, will awaken as a little babe. Born in violence, in a manger where the wild beasts eat, it will grow in wisdom and power as the outer you will, become passive and powerless. But, you must be watchful and vigilant of your thoughts in order to bring the outer you into passivity. Only then will you know what it is like to be in the world but not of it. The purpose of this teaching is to awaken the Christ who is asleep in man, dreaming different states into being, and bring him to the conscious circle of humanity where man is self-aware. Once you are aware of your true self, you will no longer condemn sleeping man. You will know they are machines, automatons who do not know what they are doing.

Your desires are not subjective, intangible things, but solidly real. Begin to awaken the Christ in you by clothing your subjective desires in objective reality. I promise you, the day you do this, they will become facts in your world. Have an aim that you will not lie to yourself anymore. Work on this feature within yourself. Become extremely observant and honest with yourself and watch the energy that formerly moved into negative states, flow into your greater aim. Perhaps your aim is to become a great teacher, not because you want to impose your will upon others, but because you want to awaken in others what you have awakened in yourself. The awakening begins when you feel a separation; a division of the natural and the spiritual imaginative you to which all things are possible. It is this spiritual you that clothes your subjective state in reality.

By changing the feeling of "I," you can direct your life internally and escape the prison of your present state regardless of what it may be. By thinking from the point of view that the problem is solved, you move from the problem to its solution. This change of attitude is called the Be-attitudes. In other words, you are "being" what you want to be by assuming that you already are it. When you know what you want, consciously clothe yourself in a new concept of self by extracting your "I" from the evidence of the senses and placing it in the place you want to be. By this assumption (or be-attitude), you have journeyed from one state to another. "And I, if I be lifted up, I draw all men to me."

Once you have lifted yourself up into the new states abide there! Do not come back to the testimonies of your, senses, but remain in your desire until a different world is established. Every change in the feeling of "I" automatically produces changes in the external world; therefore, you must learn to die daily to your old beliefs. The statement, "Those who lose their life for my sake will find it," means letting go of all that you now consent to. If you lose it, you will find your "I" reclothing itself on a higher level of beings; thereby causing a new expression in your world.

When you go in a new direction, the journey is made in the mind. A physical journey may follow, but the journey must be made on the inside first. Where you are, is what you psychologically are at that moment. An enlightened being lives on the mountain top and the human imagination, when completely controlled, is personified as a being called Jesus Christ.

As long as you are violent, you are asleep. Awaken the spiritual you by watching your actions and reactions to life, and you will lose your impulse to retaliate. What happens to you here is not important, but how you react to what happens, is. Your reactions define you. They tell you where you are, for you attract life in its most minute detail.

The Bible does not teach reincarnation. Its central teaching is the rebirth of consciousness into ever higher and higher levels. You must be born by water and spirit, not water only. Except a man be born of the Spirit, he cannot enter the higher level of being called the kingdom of heaven. In this series of lectures, you have received psychological instruction as to how to go about working on yourself. Your mind has been washed of certain errors, baptized and born of water. But, unless this truth is applied, you will not be born of the spirit.

The word "Mary" means "water." Christ, the "I" in you, is born of water and of the Holy Spirit. The outer you cannot receive instructions. He is literal and takes things literally, thereby receiving nothing but stone. The righteous man, however, is conscious of being the man he wants to be, while the foolish man steals from himself by not claiming his desire. Every time you see a man less than what he wants to be, you have robbed him of The state necessary to externalize it.

Be not as the heathen who, by vain repetition hopes he can get the ear of God. Rather, when you pray, go within and close the door, and your Father who hears in secret will reward you openly. You have but to change the feeling of "I." Close the door to the outer world and feel yourself into the state your friend desires. With a planned program, see him and talk to him from the premise that he is that person already. Keep the door of reason and logic closed and walk in faith that what you have heard and seen, in secret, will be rewarded openly, and it will.

The Bible was written by the conscious circle of humanity. (This circle you enter at the moment of wakefulness.) Not composed by men, the Bible is divine instruction with limitless interpretations. It is a test in the development of your understanding and, as you grow, its understanding deepens and deepens.

Although man wraps himself in conditions (states), the being he really is, is I AM. Anything man will consent to, he will manifest in his world. Can you accept as fact what your reason and senses deny? Or must you always bow to reason's dictates? The same consciousness that produces health, produces sickness, wealth or poverty. Whatever you agree to be conscious of, whatever you affirm as true, you will manifest.

When you know the spiritual being within you, you will assert the supremacy of imagination and put all things subjective to it. All knees must bow to imagination. "Behold! We are transformed into the same image." Can you behold a given situation and make it so natural that you are transformed into its image? You can when you, all imagination, feel the naturalness of the image you behold.

Divinity is not divided; therefore, everyone is but a projection of the one. You are told to love your neighbors as yourself, for there is no other. Sanctify self, not another. Working on others will not change them; only by changing yourself will the others change. Seek confirmation of your ideas and you are not growing. All textbooks are manmade and uninspired from on high. Stick to them and you will remain on their level. Believe in self! Trust your human imagination and you will grow in wisdom and in stature and, as you grow, you outgrow your former beliefs.

My ideas regarding the historicity of the Bible are not original. The Encyclopedia Biblica was published in 1888. Sponsored by Oxford University, it took twelve years for one hundred and twenty-seven brilliant minds from all faiths to complete it. These men, who knew the ancient tongues, after intense research came to the conclusion that the Bible, from cover to cover, was mythological allegory. Another wonderful book is Smith's Dictionary of the Bible. Published in 1860, it is made up of four volumes. They discovered that the writers of the Bible used a phallic frame to which they attached their psychological truths. "And when their eyes were opened, they knew him." To know, is to have union with and become what is beheld; therefore, he vanished from their sight when they knew him.

In the 3rd Chapter of 1st John, he tells us, "See what love the Father has given us that we should be called children of God, and so we are. The world does not know us because it does not know him. As God's children, it does not yet appear what we shall be, but we know that when he appears, we shall be like him, for we shall see him as he is. Everyone who hopes in him, purifies himself, as he is pure."

We are God's children, destined to be God himself, and God creates everything he, individualized as you, consents to. Therefore, resolve only to hear what is good concerning yourself and another. If you adopt this attitude, everything that enters your mind will contribute to a noble life and you will discover the joy of feasting on higher states.

When a man dies, it is an expansion into a dimensionally larger life. If you have not awakened here, you must start awakening in the fourth dimension. Climbing a multitudinous dimensional time block, you ascend by reason of your ability to function in a dimensionally larger world. And each dimensional world is contained in a dimensionally larger world; in turn that world is contained in a still dimensionally larger world without end. But, remembering the love the Father has given you, test him, knowing that everyone who hopes in him, purifies himself as he is pure.

www.ingramcontent.com/pod-product-compliance
Lightning Source LLC
LaVergne TN
LVHW041707070526
838199LV00045B/1244